Praise for The Traffic Power Structure and Planka.nu

"The group's efficiency in evasion has created an enviable business model."
—Matt Flegenheimer, *New York Times*

"We could build a Berlin Wall around the metro stations, and they would still try to find ways to get around it."
—Jesper Pettersson, spokesperson for Stockholm's Public Transport Services

"Not a sentence without a message, not a word in the wrong place."
—Lars Wilderäng, Cornucopia

"Well written, well informed, and well conceived."
—Swedish Arts Council

"Scandinavia might seem an unlikely breeding ground for a subway revolution."
—*Wall Street Journal*

The
Traffic
Power
Structure

Planka.nu

Translated by Gabriel Kuhn

PM Press 2016

The Traffic Power Structure
Planka.nu

ISBN: 978-1-62963-1-530
Library of Congress Control Number: 2016930968

Cover by John Yates/Stealworks
Layout by Jonathan Rowland
Translated by Gabriel Kuhn
Illustrations by Felix Hetscher (with thanks to UNRAST-Verlag,
        www.unrast-verlag.de)

10 9 8 7 6 5 4 3 2 1

PM Press
PO Box 23912
Oakland, CA 94623
www.pmpress.org

Printed in the USA by the Employee Owners of Thomson-Shore in
Dexter, Michigan. www.thomsonshore.com

Contents

The Traffic Power Structure

You're not born a motorist, you become one.

Mobility and class are tightly linked. Not only because mobility depends on economic resources but also because a society based on the current mobility paradigm—what we call *automobility*—contributes directly to the increase of economic and social injustice.

It is self-evident that a society prioritizing automobile traffic benefits motorists. It is also true that affluent white men are overrepresented among motorists. A society that prioritizes automobile traffic and sees mobility as a magical recipe for progress sharpens the contradictions between individuals and social groups.

The traffic power structure establishes a hierarchy among different means of transport. The automobile comes out on top. At the bottom we find pedestrians, bicyclists, and public transport. The resources allocated to different means of transport reflect this hierarchy. The superiority of the automobile is the result of a society guided by the principle of automobility, that is, a society in which the automobile gets to define our existence.

This book was written to shed light on the traffic power structure and its consequences. A society based on automobility is not only ecologically unsustainable but also leads to economic and social segregation. Investigating current transport policies while outlining different ones can, in our opinion, contribute to solutions for many social problems.

Automobile traffic turns us into competitors. Who has never felt turning into a bona fide motorist once he or she sits down behind the wheel? Driving a car seems to lead to egotistical behavior almost inevitably. Everyone tries to win at the cost of others. Our fellow human beings—other drivers, cyclists, pedestrians, and the passengers in public transport—turn into obstacles. Let's be honest: who has never personally felt the aggressiveness and the competitive egoism caused by the automobile? Since we don't want to encourage such behavior and are convinced that you're not born a motorist but become one, our aim is to end this particular chapter of human evolution. This requires not only changing the traffic power structure and removing the automobile from its pedestal but also building a society that is based on other principles: a society where no one is forced to participate in the traffic power structure, neither actively nor passively; a society where the satisfaction of human needs and desires comes first; a society that we create together and in which we live together; a society consisting of (local) *societies*.

Automobility

First, the term *automobility* refers to all of the institutions and practices that determine the social role of the automobile.

Second, it emphasizes this role. Finally, it refers to the discourses that make the automobile the social engine of our time and associate it with freedom, progress, movement, individuality, and independence. The automobile is the socio-technological cornerstone of modernity.

The term *automobility* is a compound noun bringing together *autonomy* and *mobility*—the wordplay with *auto* in the beginning gives it a nice twist. Today, it seems as if autonomy can only be realized through mobility, and mobility only through autonomy. Automobility is closely linked to the ideology of liberalism, which emphasizes our role as individuals with freedom of choice and, in the most extreme case, questions the existence of society altogether. The notion of the free individual is produced by a certain form of society, and so is the notion of automobility. Without roads, oil, and the auto industry no one could drive a car. But the notion of automobility is an internal contradiction. Motorists drive on roads planned by technocrats and move between residential areas and workplaces whose locations are selected according to economic interests. There really isn't much free choice.

It is indeed strange that the automobile of all things has become the ultimate symbol of freedom and individuality. The truth is that the automobile belongs to the Holy Grail of modern liberalism: it is subjected to a plenitude of public and private techniques of control. Numerous regulations are required for the automobile society to function: how fast you are allowed to drive, where you are allowed to drive, which direction you are allowed to drive, where you are allowed to park, what amount of emissions you are allowed to discharge, and which risks you are allowed to take. These regulations, and many more, need to be considered whenever you start the engine. In order to enforce them, an apparatus of control disciplines motorists and nonmotorists alike. The alleged freedom of the road correlates to a strict control of movement.

The automobility regime is characterized by a number of immanent, unsolvable, and destructive tendencies. Mass traffic means congestion. While automobility encourages individual use of the automobile, it turns into *im*mobility as soon as people follow the encouragement. Traffic congestion is not an anomaly of the automobile society but its logical consequence. The biggest enemy of mass traffic is mass traffic itself. While mass traffic is required for the image of the motorist's freedom to shine, it is mass traffic that denies this very freedom.

Mass traffic also means destruction: the climate, our natural resources, our cities, we as human beings, and indeed the entire geopolitical system are affected by acute crises. Climate change is an inescapable overtone to the humming of the engines. The residents of our cities are robbed of their space. Peak oil creates geopolitical crises, even wars, as access to cheap oil must be secured. Every year, 1.2 million people die in traffic crashes.[1]

Again, we are not talking about temporary disruptions of a system working fine otherwise. The exact opposite is true: what we describe is the system's normality. The roads and the cars that have been built for automobility to prosper kill three thousand people every day. But when was the last time we heard a politician criticize mass traffic? Given the current political climate it seems unthinkable that any politician would dare declare war on the automobile. Yes, in Sweden we have "Vision Zero," that is, the aim not to have a single person killed

---

1   Steffen Böhm, Campbell Jones, Chris Land, and Matthew Paterson, "Impossibilities of Automobility," introduction to Steffen Böhm, Campbell Jones, Chris Land, and Matthew Paterson, eds., *Against Automobility* (Malden, MA: Blackwell, 2006), 9–10.

in traffic, but this vision is little more than a paper tiger. This is hardly surprising when people try to relieve the symptoms of a problem while ignoring its causes. The traffic deaths are a *political* problem, but no one sees it that way. It is as if we have surrendered to murderous machines taking over our planet.

It is obvious that in its practical implementation, automobility is not functioning and far from rational. The notion's inadequacy is also revealed on a theoretical level. Automobility as a system is an impossibility. What is celebrated as a way to freedom and autonomy rests on a tight-knit net of control.

The idea of automobility is directly linked to mass traffic but it also characterizes many other parts of society. If we use the term correctly, it is an excellent tool for analyzing society as a whole, but also for creating radical alternatives, both social and ecological. The term helps us understand the idea of the modern individual and the possibilities (and limits) of his or her movement. The myth of the free and autonomous individual often makes it hard to see these connections, which makes the attempt to disclose them even more urgent.

In order to illustrate the potentials of the term automobility as an analytical tool, let us turn to the concept of the podcar. In Sweden, the podcar is often promoted as a solution to those aspects of automobile traffic that many see as problematic: emissions and urban decay. Essentially, the podcar attempts to solve these problems by adapting public transport to the needs of automobility. But how is this going to solve anything? After all, it is exactly these needs that create the problems. In the best case, the podcar motivates some motorists not to drive their car every day. But is this going to change the structure of our cities? Hardly.[2]

It is especially Greens and Liberals who—in an ominous union with companies profiting from personal rapid transit—beat the advertising drum. This is not surprising. It shows how deeply rooted the liberal conviction of separating the individual from society has become. It also illustrates the difficulty of conceiving mobility as a political problem, even if the influence of transport on our lives is striking. Still, problems of traffic are primarily seen as technological problems. Their solutions are left to engineers, no matter the close ties between the political economy of movement and questions of urban development, climate, environment, energy, justice, equality, migration, and accumulation of capital. The traffic power structure determines not only the relationship between car and bus but also between human being and human being. The question of traffic, and of human movement in general, is too important to be left to politicians, corporations, and so-called experts. It is a question that must engage all of us.

---

2   For podcar advocates, see the website www.podcar.org.

Accessibility

*"Cruel town, it's a cruel town / Cold people, cruel town
Cruel town, it's a cruel town / If you fall, you stay down
Cold city, cruel system / Nothing's made for people"*
　—Broder Daniel

Now we have identified a political problem. What's next? Is there anything beyond the paradigm of automobility? We suggest replacing it with the paradigm of accessibility. Instead of vast road and rail networks, accessibility should be the guiding principle for how we plan transport and traffic.

The paradigm of accessibility suggests that all people should have access to necessary and desirable social services in the places where they live. It is an approach that subverts the idea of mobility as a value in itself. This cannot happen overnight. It requires enormous adjustments in the planning of residential areas and workplaces. In addition, automobile traffic needs to be reduced and movement by foot, bicycle, and public transport increased. Even a commission appointed by the U.S. Congress made proposals leaning in that direction. The commission recommended adding a vehicle miles traveled tax to the gas tax. This would mean that all motorists, regardless of the vehicle they drive, need to pay a fee for the distances they cover.[1]

1　National Surface Transportation Infrastructure Financing Commission, "Paying Our Way: A New Framework for Transportation Finance," 2009, http://financecommission.dot.gov/Documents/NSTIF_Commission_Final_Report_Exec_Summary_Feb09.pdf.

The proposition does not focus on emission but on usage of the automobile itself. This is an interesting development.

Interesting are also the experiences in Copenhagen, after many heavily trafficked roads were narrowed down and parking sites in the city reduced by 2 to 3 percent a year. As a result, automobile traffic was reduced, since people got an incentive to use other means of transport. The number of pedestrians, cyclists, and passengers in public transport grew in proportion to the dwindling number of motorists. Meanwhile, the urban space that was freed by the reduction of parking sites was transformed into public space in the form of pedestrian zones, bicycle lanes, squares, and outdoor cafés.[2]

There are further means to reduce automobile traffic that are concrete, cheap, and relatively easy to implement: congestion charges (under the condition that the revenues they bring are invested in public transport), car-free zones, additional lanes for buses, trolleys, and bicycles, broader sidewalks, and stricter legislation against illegal parking. Bicycle-sharing systems can be extended from the inner cities to entire urban areas, with stations at each bigger traffic junction. Public transport needs to become true public space. This would not only increase its attraction relative to automobile traffic but also establish it as a counter-pole to the automobility paradigm altogether. While the automobile defines a private space in which every traffic participant is an obstacle, the quality of public transport as a social space increases with the number of people using it. If we can make public transport free of charge, and hence accessible to everyone, this social aspect would be emphasized.

---

2   Jan Gehl and Lars Gemzøe, *Public Spaces, Public Life* (Copenhagen: Danish Architectural Press, 2004), 40–41.

We stress the social aspects of public transport because we enjoy sharing our lives with other people, but also because a lively public space is a requirement for people to feel safe. We envision a public transport system that reflects the diversity of the society we live and move in and that constitutes a space that is inviting to all.

At this point, we have not only identified a political problem but have also outlined ways to reduce automobile traffic for the benefit of ecologically and socially sustainable means of transport. But this does not answer the crucial question about the structural changes necessary to move from the paradigm of mobility to the paradigm of accessibility.

First of all, it must be clear that nothing about the current traffic situation is "natural" or "necessary." The traffic power structure is the result of political decisions. All the billions invested in motorways could just as well be invested in public transport. Slogans like There Is No Alternative are nonsense. The opportunity to make different decisions always exists. Yet nothing will change as long as those responsible will not stop the private interests that destroy our social relationships. If we want to change things, we must focus on local communities destroyed by mass traffic, development plans, privatization, and social segregation. We must believe in the possibility to halt this process and in the possibility of political change. Without these beliefs there is no hope for a different kind of life.

Public transport must become a central aspect of urban planning. How often we have to travel in any given city depends on how that particular city is built. And this does not concern only the city center. Of course, city centers with fewer cars, more trolleys, more bicycle lanes, and more liveliness are nice. But how about the city's other areas? In a city like Stockholm, most people do not live in the center but in the suburbs, and it is there that social change needs to begin. The middle classes in the city centers will always manage, inspired by the likes of Jan Gehl, the famed Danish urban designer. Our attention must lie elsewhere. Yes, suburbs can be inspired by car-free city centers. But this inspiration alone will not transform our suburbs into stimulating and welcoming places. It is impossible to say how exactly this transformation will unravel. It depends on the specific circumstances. But each transformation must begin with the affected communities and their needs and desires.

In recent years, "local organizing" has become a popular slogan in Sweden. We have seen many community-based struggles. In Stockholm, the campaign Rädda Aspuddsbadet received much attention. It fought to save the public bath in the suburb of Aspudden. The plans for shutting it down were a logical consequence of the automobility paradigm: all social services are moved to designated places, while most suburbs are reduced to sleeping quarters. This is the reason why Rädda Aspuddsbadet touched such a nerve. It was about more than just saving a local bathhouse. The trigger could have been the closure of a youth or community center anywhere in Sweden.

The campaign advocated for the right of the people to be able to satisfy their needs and desires in the places where they live. It entailed a struggle against automobility insofar as it challenged the notion that people must move between places, whether by car or public transport, in order to access services. Cash machines, daycare centers, and clinics have to be available to people without them having to travel long journeys.

Fighting for seemingly small changes in the suburbs is an important first step in rejecting our dependence on transport. But there is more. The principle of automobility is also linked to class. A concentration of social services in specific places means that the upper classes will find it easier to access them than the lower ones. The principle of accessibility is essential. Everyone must be able to use social services near their homes and everyone should be involved in keeping their standards as high as possible. After all, it is only folks with higher incomes who can afford to travel to social service institutions farther afield as soon as they are dissatisfied with the local ones. When low-income communities from public housing complexes and high-income communities from single-family homes share social services, the quality improves for all.

Our suburbs need to be filled with people even when we are not moving to and from work. Lively suburbs reduce our dependence on transport and provide a sense of security that guards, steel doors, and monitoring cameras never can. People feel safe around other people; it isn't more complicated than

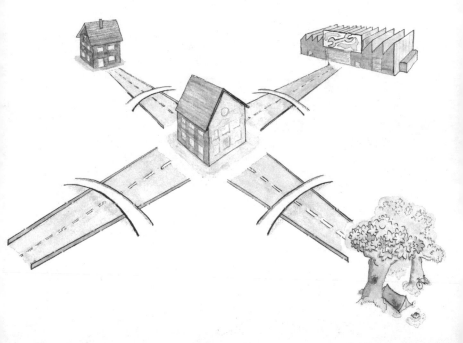

that. A city with open and attractive public space is a city full of life, and a city full of life has open and attractive public space. The way our cities are structured impacts our behavior and our relationships.

Transport must not be addressed as an issue separate from other social issues. Transport is directly linked to urban planning. How does urban planning affect everyday life? Cities with soulless transport options have a fatal effect. Segregation and alienation become unavoidable, and living creatively becomes impossible when all activities—sleeping, working, shopping, learning, having fun—have their designated place. Division of labor and separation of duties may excite bosses and bureaucrats but ruin our lives. This is a reality we need to face.

The Metropolis

"It's up to us to change this town called malice."
—The Jam

In the modern metropolis, the traffic power structure hardly ever becomes more obvious than after a snowstorm. While cars usually roll through the city as if nothing has happened, pedestrians, including those with strollers and walkers, battle it out on icy sidewalks—that is, if these are not closed due to the danger of roof avalanches and icicles. In that case, pedestrians are forced to move onto the road, where motorists show little understanding for having to share their path with others.

With respect to roads, the rules for plowing are easy. The state takes care of its roads and the municipalities of theirs. With respect to sidewalks, however, there is plenty of confusion. Sometimes the municipalities are responsible, sometimes the house owners. (The latter are also responsible for cleaning the courtyards, stairways, driveways, and roofs.)[1] Only a third of Stockholm's residents know what regulations apply to their housing block.[2] In fact, when comparing roads with sidewalks and bicycle lanes, one can get the impression that no one is responsible for pedestrians and bicyclists at all. Meanwhile, it is often impossible for people with strollers and walkers to

---

1   Catarina Håkansson, "Snöröjningen har fungerat," *Aftonbladet*, December 16, 2009, http://www.aftonbladet.se/nyheter/article6303188.ab.

2   Emma Björkman, "Snöröjning är fastighetsägarens ansvar," *Länstidningen Södertälje*, December 22, 2009, http://lt.se/nyheter/1.686446-snorojning-ar-fastighetsagarens-ansvar.

get anywhere, especially when mountains of snow have been heaped onto the sidewalk in order to clear the motorists' way.

Snowplowing serves as an excellent example of the priority of automobile traffic and the consequences of the automobility paradigm. The traffic power structure becomes a self-fulfilling prophecy: it guarantees that the roads are cleared first, which leads to even more people using cars.

Hierarchies not only exist between different means of transport but also within automobile culture itself. A society guided by just-in-time production makes itself dependent on an armada of trucks in constant motion. Commercially important roads are therefore cleared first, while access roads to public housing complexes are cleared last. Similar priorities exist in the countryside, where the dependence on private automobile use is even greater.

Illegal Parking and Fare-Dodging

In a cold and gray week in February 2010, two incidents occurred that, in combination, illustrate the traffic power structure perfectly. The first concerned a case that later became known as "Gategate," after a fellow named Jesper Nilsson had recorded two plainclothes policemen working as ticket inspectors in the Stockholm subway system.[3] The second concerned a trial in Malmö against a motorist who had attacked and threatened a parking attendant.[4]

When Jesper Nilsson saw two plainclothes policemen stop a group of youths at the gates of the Hornstull subway station

---

3   Jesper Nilsson, "Polisen som mitt i tunnelbanan står," *Tuggarna*, February 11, 2010, https://web.archive.org/web/20110425011630/ http://tuggarna.posterous.com/polisen-som-mitt-i-tunnelbanan-star.

4   "Hård kritik mot p-vaktsdom," *Svenska Dagbladet*, February 12, 2010, http:// www.svd.se/nyheter/inrikes/hard-kritik-mot-p-vaktsdom_4251117.svd.

in Stockholm, he decided to record their actions on his mobile phone. This was not appreciated by the officers. Although it is perfectly legal to record what happens in the Stockholm subway system, they threatened to take Nilsson to the police station for a urine sample if he didn't erase the recordings. The case received big media attention and the policemen were strongly criticized. But the critique focused on how they dealt with Nilsson, while hardly anyone wondered why plainclothes policemen were working as ticket inspectors in the first place. Are the police really given public resources in order to harass passengers in public transport? It is important to discuss ambiguous legal clauses—in this case, the use of drug laws as a threat—but this must not overshadow the question why a private company such as MTR, which runs the Stockholm subway system, can rely on ticket inspectors funded by taxes.

Now, what happened during that same week in the Malmö district court? A trial was scheduled against a parking violator who had choked a parking attendant and promised to chase her "until the end of her days." The court decided not to grant the parking attendant any damages because she belonged to a profession whose members "need to be prepared for such attacks."[5] In other words, instead of questioning the mechanisms that lead to specific forms of road rage and instead of holding people accountable when they hurt others, the Malmö district court demanded leniency for frustrated motorists. It seems fitting that Sweden's then center-right government canceled all funding for research on improving the working conditions of parking attendants.[6] The court's decision was a

---

5   Ibid.

6   Mikael Färnbo, "Succé för sextimmarsdag," *Arbetaren*, March 14, 2007, https://www.arbetaren.se/2007/03/14/succe-for-sextimmarsdag/.

bow to automobile traffic and motorists' interests. Leniency for parking violators is a logical consequence of the traffic power structure. It apparently does not suffice to reserve a tremendous percentage of our public space for parking; we must also tolerate that some motorists insist on parking illegally anyway.

How is it that policemen act as ticket inspectors in the subway, while judges show leniency toward parking violators? It is important to ask this question. The problem, of course, goes beyond policemen harassing subway passengers instead of booking parking violators. The Malmö ruling shows how prevalent such priorities are. And politicians confirm it, too. In Stockholm, illegal parking will cost you between 475 and 900 crowns. The fine for riding public transport without a valid ticket is 1,200 crowns. Essentially, this means that automobile traffic is subsidized. Even people opposed to fare-dodging cannot possibly argue that it causes more damage than illegal parking. People who ride public transport without a ticket often belong to low-income classes and depend on fare-dodging for moving around. The parking violator, on the other hand, is often a rich man who thinks that he can park his Mercedes wherever he wants; and if people dare challenge him, he thinks he has the right to offend or abuse them.[7] The parking violator may endanger others even if he doesn't attack anyone personally, as he forces pedestrians onto the road or blocks the way for emergency vehicles.

---

7   See Moa Stridde, "Porscheägare i topp bland felparkerare," *Metro*, May 30, 2008, http://www.metro.se/nyheter/porscheagare-i-topp-bland-felparkerare/ObjheD!07_1828-65/; "83-åring slog ner 99-åring," *Aftonbladet*, January 23, 2010, http://www.aftonbladet.se/nyheter/article6476541.ab; "Hotfull felparkerare åtalad för misshandel," *Nyheter P4 Jönköping*, February 16, 2009, http://sverigesradio.se/sida/artikel.aspx?programid=91&artikel=2639663.

If we compare the millions of crowns invested in new barriers and controls in public transport with the disinterest for illegal parking, the traffic power structure becomes painfully obvious. If politicians took illegal parking only nearly as seriously as fare-dodging, they would have long ago made means available to build safer bicycle lanes and sidewalks, and they would tow illegally parked cars or put wheel clamps on them. But no one seems interested in this. You don't want to mess with the auto-industrial complex. It is much easier to vilify fare-dodgers as "parasites" and have them harassed by ticket inspectors, security guards—and police officers.

Road Rage

Road rage is a logical consequence of the behavior enforced upon people by automobile traffic. In principle, each anger attack in the context of automobile traffic should be considered a form of road rage. At the same time, there is a difference between road rage and the anger that nonmotorists might feel toward cars. The latter should rather be called "car hatred." The act of an SUV driver who honks and yells at a pensioner whom he considers to be crossing the road too slowly is not comparable to a pensioner pouring sugar into the tank of an SUV under the cover of darkness.

Mette Møller, who works at the Institute for Transport of the Technical University of Denmark, notes that the most common reasons for road rage are "traffic congestion, waiting at traffic lights, and delays caused by others."[8] All of these circumstances belong to the normality of mass traffic. In Denmark,

8   "Vrede forhindrer bilister i at køre sikkert," *Trafiksikkerhedsforskning. Nyhetsbrev från DTU Transport, Danmarks Tekniske Universitet,* vol. 8, 2009, http://www.trafiksikkerhedsforskning.dk/Default.aspx?id=337.

where road rage seems widespread, the phenomenon has been researched for a long time. Dramatic and disturbing statistics emerge: "During a twelve-month period, 19,550 people were physically attacked by other traffic participants and 169,334 were threatened. In Australia, it is assumed that up to 91 percent of all cases of road rage are never reported to the police."[9]

Based on the international studies Møller refers to, the effects of road rage extend far beyond the consequences suffered by the victims of physical aggression. Road rage leads not only to intended physical attacks but also to accidents. According to Møller, road rage derives from the reification of others, a process implied in automobile traffic:

> Driving a car puts you in a very special position. The kind of social interaction you engage in differs essentially from most social interaction in everyday life. When people jump the queue in a supermarket, you are able to get an impression of them; for example, you might see a facial expression. This is not the case in car traffic. It is difficult to know why other drivers behave the way they do or whether they behave so consciously or not. This has two consequences: first, misunderstandings come very easily; second, other traffic participants are seen as anonymous figures ("the woman driving the red Ford") instead of individuals in a social context ("the tired and sad woman on the way to visit her mother in the hospital"). It is much easier to live out aggression in car traffic because the affected people hardly ever have a chance to react.[10]

---

9   Ibid.

10   Mette Møller, "Hvad ved vi om vejvrede?," *Dansk Vejtidsskrift*, vol. 1, 2007, http://asp.vejtid.dk/Artikler/2007/01%5C4864.pdf.

Some researchers, politicians, and other know-it-alls claim that road rage can be explained "genetically," but we are interested neither in amateur psychology nor in vulgar genetics. No proper discussion about road rage can be had without considering the social conditions that make it possible.

It is not surprising that many people want to reduce road rage to a personality disorder. This allows them to employ pseudo-measures, for example the treatment of "a few bad apples," while ignoring the problem's true causes. Blinders of this kind are very convenient for denying the politics of mass traffic. But if we really want to grasp the road rage phenomenon, the political underpinnings must not be ignored. The egotistical behavior expressed in road rage has to be understood as a consequence of the overall behavior that car traffic inevitably leads to.

Just as traffic congestion, road rage cannot be seen as a simple abnormality of an otherwise well-functioning system. Road rage is not the result of a "few nutcases" acting out. Any such claim would be as ridiculous as the claim that the latest crisis in capitalism was the result of a few bankers' greed. Mette Møller is right when she says that "less traffic congestion would make a difference," but that the solution of the problem as a whole is "far more complicated."[11]

Parking Tales I

Illegal parking is far from the only problem related to parking. Parking lanes, parking lots, and parking garages must all be analyzed through the traffic power structure. The "parking power structure" reveals two lines of conflict: those between different means of transport and those within automobile culture itself.

---

11 Ibid.

A motorist claims up to one thousand times more "space time" (the time that a certain space is used) than a passenger in public transport. Parking takes up by far the greatest amount of space time.[12]

The automobile is unique in its need for parking. Neither pedestrians nor passengers in public transport need parking space, and bicyclists only need a minimal one. Of course, the vehicles used in public transport must be parked on occasion, but the space they require only makes up a fraction of the space necessary to park all private vehicles. Furthermore, when planned wisely, parking spaces for public transport vehicles don't get in the way of everyday life.

Not only the automobile's need for parking is unique; it is also unique how mandatory it seems for politicians to meet this need. This proves the automobile's status as the master of the traffic power structure. The public space allocated to the automobile is phenomenal. One of the main arguments against expanding Stockholm's bicycle-sharing system is lack of space. There are lending stations ready to be installed, and the number of available bicycles could be doubled overnight. But for this to happen, 0.3 percent of the parking space dedicated to cars would have to be made available—0.3 percent! Alas, the automobile is untouchable. It cannot be deprived of its parking space.[13]

On a regular day, people use their cars to drive to and from work and maybe take a swing to the shopping mall or the gym.

12 Anders Gullberg, Olle Hagman, and Per Lundin, *Stockholmsparkering: Mellan allas nytta och individuellt förtret* (Stockholm: Stockholmia, 2007), 103–4.
13 "Miljöpartiet kräver att Moderaterna agerar i frågan om lånecyklar," *Pressmeddelande från Miljöpartiet de gröna*, April 14, 2010, http://www.mynewsdesk.com/se/miljopartiet-i-stockholms-stad/pressreleases/miljoepartiet-kraever-att-moderaterna-agerar-i-fraagan-om-laanecyklar-735033.

For the well-being of the motorists, we hope that most of them do not spend more than two or three hours per day in their car. The rest of the time—more than twenty hours—the car is parked. It causes damage all day. We usually don't perceive it that way since we focus on emission. However, a parked car still threatens the city and the diversity of human relationships in it.

Parking Tales II

In their book *Lots of Parking*, John A. Jakle and Keith A. Sculle explain how parking turns places into nonplaces:

> Visually exciting landscapes with temporal depth, as architectural historian James Marston Fitch argued, offered residents and visitors a strong sense of place. . . . Certainly, widened streets and new city freeways broke up traditional cityscapes and hastened the decline of the pedestrian-orientation of cities. But nothing fragmented urban space more than the parking lot. In the half century between 1920 and 1970, most traditional big city downtowns substantially unraveled—disemboweled, building by building, by expanses of parking lot asphalt.[14]

In this sense, the parking space is the antithesis to the building; it is an anti-building. A parking space creates no new place but relies on the destruction of a place. Parking spaces tear cities apart and follow a logic of uniformity, which makes the urban landscape increasingly homogeneous; all difference is flattened and the rule of the nonplace takes hold.

---

14 John A. Jakle and Keith A. Sculle, *Lots of Parking: Land Use in a Car Culture* (Charlottesville: University of Virginia Press, 2005), 8.

In his book *Place and Placelessness,* the geographer Edward Relph describes the nonplaces created by the need for parking as "simple landscapes": "The simple landscape declares itself openly, presents not problems or surprises, lacks subtlety; there are none of the ambiguities and contradictions and complexities that . . . lend meaning to building and man-made environments; there are no deep significances, only a turning to the obvious and a separation of different functions into distinct units."[15]

The parking space is a prime example for the separation of duties: if it is used for something other than parking, it loses its purpose.

The word *parking* derives from the Latin *parricus,* which means "enclosed place." That the word *park* also derives from *parricus* is ironic: *parricus* gave way to a word signifying a place of trees, grass, and life, and to a word signifying the exact opposite.

Parking has a high price. It not only destroys places but is also expensive. There really is no "free parking." Rather, the costs for parking are outsourced: we find them in higher rents and higher prices for land and real estate, they make goods in stores more expensive, and they demand challenges for urban planning because of lower residential density. Motorists may sometimes pay for parking—but we collectively pay for it all the time.[16]

The subsidies for parking are among the biggest problems of our cities. They not only fortify automobile traffic but also

15 Ibid., 96.
16 Ragnar Hedström and Tomas Svensson, "Parkering: Politik, åtgärder och konsekvenser för stadstrafik," *Rapport från Statens väg- och transportforskningsinstitut* (VTI), 2010, http://www.vti.se/EPiBrowser/Publikationer/N23-2010.pdf.

raise living costs for nonmotorists. In Stockholm, only one of twenty commuters pays the effective costs of the parking space their vehicle requires. Of the average net wage of Stockholm's residents, 5 percent is invested in providing "free parking." It has been estimated that if all motorists were forced to cover the full cost of their parking needs, the number of commuters would instantly drop by as much as 20 percent.[17] Instead, construction companies are required to build a certain amount of parking spots with every new building, depending on the building's size and purpose. The relevant regulations were further sharpened in 2008. *More parking spaces per building!* has become the rallying cry of the city government.[18] In practice this means—besides additional parking spaces and cars—higher living costs for all. Construction costs for a single parking spot in a parking garage can be as high as 400,000 crowns. As we have seen, it is hardly ever the motorists who carry the costs. Rather, the costs are divided between all local residents, no matter whether they own a car or not.

A parking spot exists for one purpose only. It doesn't matter whether a car is occupying it or not; it must not be used for anything else, otherwise it loses its purpose as an exclusive storage space. A parking spot can be occupied or unoccupied, but it is always a parking spot. And when it is occupied, it can be occupied by only one car. Meanwhile, lively cities demand places that are not reduced to one purpose only; they require places where new things can happen. In the modern city, there is an acute lack of such places—unregulated places whose purpose

17 Gullberg, Hagman, and Lundin, 174.

18 Anders Gardebring, "City skriver om parkeringsnormen," *Yimby*, March 10, 2008, http://www.yimby.se/2008/03/city-skriver-om-parkering_500.html.

is not determined, stimulating places where the unexpected can happen. It is mind-boggling how much space not occupied by buildings and roads is reserved for idle cars.

In many cities in the world, PARK(ing) Day is celebrated. On PARK(ing) Day, people occupy parking spaces and turn them into parks.[19] The day's significance goes beyond a clever play on words, and also beyond taking space away from motorists. What matters are the consequences: some parking spaces are turned into gardens, others are used for setting up hammocks and for playing music, and others still become picnic spots. Whatever the outcome, the transformations demonstrate how monotonous these (non)places usually are and how much potential they have once the monotony is disrupted.

Under the parking lot, the city.

---

19 See the website www.parkingday.org.

State and Capital Travel in the Same Car

"Being totally sexual, incapable of cerebral or aesthetic responses, totally materialistic and greedy, the male, besides inflicting on the world 'Great Art,' has decorated his unlandscaped cities with ugly buildings (both inside and out), ugly decors, billboards, highways, cars, garbage trucks, and, most notably, his own putrid self."
—Valerie Solanas

It is impossible to understand the triumph of the automobile without shedding some light on the connections between state and capital. Let us take a look at history. In a thesis titled *Bilsamhället* (Automobile Society), the historian of technology Per Lundin quotes the civil engineer Stig Nordqvist, who offered the following summary of the impact of the automobile on Swedish cities: "The advent of the car in Swedish cities caused serious problems in the form of traffic congestion and accidents. The streets were not made for car traffic and there were no parking spaces. Cars had to fight their way through ever greater chaos."[1]

Already in 1955, Nordqvist had stated in the magazine *Industria* that society was not prepared for the automobile. The solution he proposed was to transform Swedish society into an automobile society. Half a century later, this has come true;

---

1   Per Lundin, *Bilsamhället: ideologi, expertis och regelskapande i efterkrigstidens Sverige* (Stockholm: Stockholmia, 2008), 17.

today we live in an automobile society, but this hasn't solved any problems. Congestion still exists, and even if the relative number of collisions has been reduced, they have in no way disappeared. Car traffic still kills, in the form of crashes as well as emissions and environmental destruction. And in many other countries the situation is even worse than in Sweden.

How did this happen? Why do we live in an automobile society? The answers we get to these questions depend on who we ask. Scholars seem to agree that the politicians of the 1950s were overwhelmed by the explosion of mass traffic. This does not mean that they ignored it. To the contrary, much was done to ring in the age of the automobile: automobile taxes were introduced, the road network was nationalized, and speed limits were softened. Yet no one seemed prepared for the consequences of these measures, namely the further acceleration of mass traffic itself.[2]

While politicians reacted to these developments, they hadn't planned them. Capitalists had. Per Lundin reveals the connections between the auto industry, the oil companies, the road construction companies, the big trading chains, and relevant interest groups. After World War II, the Swedish auto lobby consisted of about fifty powerful groups, which acted in unison. A particularly important role was played by Svenska Vägföreningen, the Association for Sweden's Roads, founded in 1914. It was perfectly suited to publicly represent the auto lobby, since it could hide the lobby's interests behind a veil of objective professionalism and technical expertise. Lundin writes:

> The network around *Svenska Vägföreningen* united scholars, businessmen, politicians, and interest groups who, in one way or another, had an investment in roads. *Svenska*

---

2   Ibid., 21.

Vägföreningen paved the way for the government's "Road
Plan for Sweden" (*Vägplan för Sverige*, SOU 1958:1), which
was adopted by parliament with a big majority in 1959. This
initiated a process of upgrading and modernizing during
which the Swedish road system was massively expanded in
order to satisfy the demands of mass traffic.[3]

The collaboration between state, capital, and interest groups
was characteristic of postwar Sweden and is often seen as a
pillar of the "Swedish model." In less flattering words it was a
form of corporatism, resting on the idea of a common social
interest whose satisfaction would benefit all sectors of society.
The automobile society, however, was never a common social
interest. There have always been winners and losers, and the
biggest winners were the corporations benefiting from it.

   According to Lundin, one of the reasons why so few people
questioned the expansion of car traffic was that "experts" were
very skilled in disguising all political problems and addressing
only "technical" ones. This paved the way for the current hegem-
ony of the car. The question has always been *how* we can adapt
our society to the automobile, and never *why* we should do so.

   At the peak of the Swedish economic boom in the 1950s,
Sweden had the biggest number of cars per capita in all of
Europe. Social democracy, which had long been very reserved,
was now fully committed to the automobile society and integrated it into their project of the "people's home" (*folkhemmet*).
A car for each man (yes, *man*) meant social justice. The trade
unions gave their unrelenting support, especially the metal-
workers' union, which hoped for new jobs resulting from the
common cause made by the state, science, capital, and the

3   Ibid., 23.

workers' movement. Thus, the consensus for mass traffic that prevails to this day was established.[4]

When a big majority in Swedish parliament decided to switch to right-hand traffic in 1963, emulating the "American dream" became more important than ever. After all, developments in the United States were the ultimate proof for the automobile's triumphal procession. The auto lobby sent technocrats and industrialists across the Atlantic for inspirational visits. When they returned, they confirmed that the age of the automobile was inevitable. It apparently never occurred to them that the American triumph of the automobile was far from a fairy tale but the result of a secret war against public transport, known as the "Great American streetcar scandal." With the help of more or less secret subsidiary companies, the American auto industry, with General Motors at its head, had bought and destroyed the public transport system of many cities in order to eliminate all possible obstacles to establishing the automobile's all-encompassing rule.[5]

In Sweden, it seemed natural to integrate the interests of the automobile society into the construction boom engulfing the country in the 1960s. Both inner cities and suburbs were restructured for the benefit of the car. The spirit of the time is perhaps best captured by the report *Stadsbyggnad, Chalmers: Arbetsgruppen för Trafiksäkerhet* (City Building, Chalmers: Working Group for Traffic Safety), better known as SCAFT and published in 1968 by the Chalmers University of Technology in Gothenburg. The report had been commissioned by the Swedish government for the purpose of increasing traffic safety.

---

4   Ibid., 25–27.

5   Bianca Mugyenyi and Yves Engler, *Stop Signs: Cars and Capitalism on the Road to Economic, Social and Ecological Decay* (Vancouver: RED/Black Point: Fernwood, 2011), 160–63.

This was certainly a noble cause, but the outcome was puzzling: rather than recommending a reduction of traffic, further structural adaptations to meet the automobile's demands were proposed. SCAFT did include ideas on how to increase traffic safety, but none of them gave much result. Given the authors' assumptions, this is hardly surprising. SCAFT could be seen as the ultimate handbook for traffic development only because it presumed that any improvement of the automobile society had to be based on further investment in it.[6]

SCAFT fitted perfectly a society with a powerful auto industry, a construction boom, and an economic wheel that spun faster by the day. The report gave everyone an official free pass to further expand the automobile society without having to consider the consequences. One thing is clear: the automobile society is never finished. All attempts to bring it to perfection over the last decades only led to further expansion: roads became even bigger, cars even more numerous, speeds even higher, and profits even more obscene. Whether any of these attempts actually made anything better didn't seem of anyone's concern; neither were questions of democracy and participation.

In the 1980s, there were strong protests against the building of a motorway along Sweden's west coast. The motorway was built nonetheless. It was a part of the so-called Scandinavian Link, a route supposed to connect Germany with Norway. The Scandinavian Link was an invention of the lobby organization European Roundtable of Industrialists (ERT), which counts the CEOs of Volvo, Fiat, and Renault among its members. The Scandinavian working group that was supposed to clear all legal obstacles included the Volvo CEO Pehr G. Gyllenhammar and the Social Democratic politician Sven Hulterström. It had the

6   Lundin, *Bilsamhället*, 230–63.

support of all Scandinavian governments. The Nordic Council later confirmed that Gyllenhammar's maneuvers behind closed doors were decisive for the then prime minister Olof Palme and his government to approve the project. The Öresund Bridge between Copenhagen and Malmö belongs to the Scandinavian Link and was also built amid strong public protest; the majority of the Social Democratic Party's rank and file were against building the bridge, but the party leadership disregarded their opposition.[7]

There are many other unpopular road construction projects, such as Förbifart Stockholm, a planned bypass of the capital city. There are numerous indications that politicians are very generous with the truth when presenting supposed facts—mainly figures— to convince the population of the projects' necessity. And let's not even get into the bailouts that politicians in different countries have granted the auto industry—we are talking about enormous sums of money, which could have easily been used to transform the entire traffic system into something much more humane.

While politicians love to make promises about climate-smart traffic policies, the automobile society keeps on rolling (and smiling). Its permanent growth still seems inevitable, despite all the problems that today are undeniable. But, as mentioned before, car traffic is not a question of technological development or a manifestation of natural law; car traffic is politics. Had politicians not made common cause with capital, we would never be where we are today.

Don't Mourn, Consume!

Soon after the Twin Towers in New York collapsed, the reigning U.S. president, George W. Bush, had an interesting advice

---

7   Lars Henriksson, *Slutkört* (Stockholm: Ordfront, 2011), 62–64.

for his people: they should go out and consume. After all, the terrorists were not to succeed in slowing down the treadmills of the economy. This says a lot about the "war on terror," which was proclaimed at the same time. It was a war meant to protect the global flow of capital, goods, and information, plus the institutions that this flow relies on: harbors, cities, airports, sea routes, railway lines, storehouses. But it is not only terrorists who threaten the rhythm of capitalist accumulation. Others do so as well: people participating in democratic uprisings, social movements blocking railway lines and airports, trade unions calling for strikes. At a conference on the "protection of the circulation of goods, services, and data," the chairman of the Swedish government's defense committee declared matter-of-factly that there were people "doing different things we don't condone";[8] he didn't just mean illegal things but anything that didn't please him and his committee.

It is not surprising that we are constantly faced with new laws protecting capital's flow, all of which are justified by the "war on terror." The powerful are worried about the instability in the Middle East, have anti-terrorist units chasing activists who sabotage the transport of nuclear waste, and undermine the right to strike in the transport sector with references to the "necessity to uphold public services."[9] And while ever more energy is needed to maintain the flow of capital, walls are built

8   Peter Hultqvist, "Hållbarheten är eftersatt! Hur försvarar vi våra flöden?," *Lecture at Folk och Försvar & Säkerhets- och försvarsföretagen,* July 8, 2011, http://www.folkochforsvar.se/index.php/fof-play-filmvisare/items/hallbarheten-aer-eftersatt-hur-foersvarar-vi-vara-floeden.

9   Shawne McKeown, "Province Makes TTC Essential Service, Strikes Now Banned," *CityNews.ca,* March 30, 2011, http://www.citynews.ca/2011/03/30/province-makes-ttc-essential-service-strikes-now-banned/.

to curtail human migration. Nothing makes the true purpose of "free mobility" more obvious. But why is the flow of capital so important, and why are even the smallest disruptions seen as such a threat?

In the second volume of *Capital*, Karl Marx explains how the time needed for capital's turnover determines a company's profit. The period of turnover is defined as "the interval of time between one circuit period of the entire capital-value and the next, the periodicity in the process of life of capital or, if you like, the time of the renewal, the repetition, of the process of self-expansion, or production, of one and the same capital-value."[10] The faster the period of turnover, the higher the profit. In his book *Spaces of Global Capitalism*, geographer David Harvey states: "We see many innovations designed to speed up production, marketing and consumption. Since distance is measured in terms of time and cost of movement, there is also intense pressure to reduce the frictions of distance by innovations in transportation and communications . . . a basic law of capital accumulation."[11]

Securing the flow of capital is one of the main tasks of the modern nation-state. If we don't consider this in our analysis, it is difficult to understand the true idea of automobility and the automobile society related to it. Behind each traffic jam hide the interests of capital, and maintaining capital's flow is one of the strongest motives for the high-speed society, the age of transport, and the security-industrial complex—phenomena we will explore in the following chapters.

---

10 Karl Marx, *Capital, Vol. II* (Moscow: Progress Publishers, 1956, based on the revised second edition in 1893, first edition 1885), quoted from https://www.marxists.org/archive/marx/works/1885-c2/ch07.htm.

11 David Harvey, *Spaces of Global Capitalism: Towards a Theory of Uneven Geographical Development* (London: Verso, 2006), 100.

The Age of Transport

"The need of a constantly expanding market for its products chases the bourgeoisie over the entire surface of the globe. It must nestle everywhere, settle everywhere, establish connections everywhere."
—Karl Marx & Friedrich Engels

The term "age of transport" was introduced by the librarian Desiré Bååk in the "Encyclopedia of the Future," edited by the journal *Glänta*. Bååk defines the age of transport thus:

A historical era (ca. 1850–2020) characterized by a feverish circulation of human beings and goods. The era was introduced by different technological innovations (steam engine, combustion engine, railway, etc.) that allowed the transportation of physical entities much faster than before. Soon, transport and the principle of mobility became purposes in themselves, veiled by terms such as "free trade," "holiday," "international exchange," and "globalization." The strongest expression of this principle ("traveling for traveling's sake") were the journeys to the moon at the end of the twentieth century and to Mars shortly before the end of the era in 2020. "Neither before nor after did anyone undertake such meaningless journeys," H. Läckberg wrote in his treatise *Das Transportalter* (2026). The end of the era was caused by the recombustion machine and a collective travel-weariness. The pointlessness of what had long been seen as a privilege suddenly became clear. This has often been regarded as the consequence of a 2015 agreement by the United Nations . . . which no longer made traveling a privilege of the upper classes.[1]

After the publication of *Glänta*'s "Future Encyclopedia," bloggers at *Copyriot* elaborated on the term "age of transport," but it seems that it was soon forgotten. We find this unfortunate, as we consider it well-suited to signify the absurdity of the obsession with transport that is so characteristic of our time.

The folks from *Copyriot* seem to have been impressed by Bååk not letting the age of transport end in a catastrophe despite peak oil. This is because of the recombustion machine that the current climate and natural resource crisis are bound to spawn: "This innocent term points at a non-dystopian possibility: a Bataillian possibility not focusing on asceticism but on the diversion of the universal combustion of affluence; on a transformation from fossil to solar, that is, on a combustion here and now."[2]

A combustion here and now. That sounds good. The *Copyriot* folks don't go into details, but the combustion of human instead of fossil energy (on which a combustion machine after peak oil will certainly depend) would without doubt lead to more walks and bicycle tours. In a significantly slower society without the need for permanent movement, we will have energy for all sorts of things. In fact, we will have so much more time that discussions about the virtue of indolence

---

1   Desiré Bååk, "Transportåldern," *Glänta*, vol. 3, 2008.

2   Rasmus Fleischer, "Ytterligare tre framtidsord (oljekrönet, transportåldern, avgrunda)," *Copyriot*, October 6, 2008, https://web. archive.org/web/20120126005112/http://copyriot.se/2008/10/06/ ytterligare-tre-framtidsord-oljekronet-transportaldern-avgrunda/.

would be inevitable. Wonderful! As Ivan Illich has demonstrated in his manifesto *Energy and Equity*, political choices and social relationships can only be made and established where speed is inhibited. This means that the end of the age of transport will open up unexpected possibilities for energy combustion.[3]

We have already discussed the positive aspects of a renaissance of accessibility: local social services, lively neighborhoods, and less meaningless transport. Without strong social movements, however, we won't get there. Only social movements can prevent a catastrophe after peak oil and ensure that the necessary social transformations will happen democratically and justly. The exact form that these transformations will take cannot be predicted, but there are propositions. In the magazine *Turbulence*, the climate activist Tadzio Mueller formulates two broad demands: "The first is climate justice, by which we assert that there is no way to solve the biocrisis without a massive redistribution of wealth and power—which in turn implies that the biocrisis can only be solved through collective struggle. The second is, currently for want of a better word, degrowth, which refers to the need for collectively planned economic shrinkage."[4]

This vision demands a minimization of the destructive aspects of an economic system that forces us to work and be on the move constantly. Already in the nineteenth century, Paul Lafargue stated the following in his essay "The Right to Be Lazy": "Our epoch has been called the century of work. It

---

3   Ivan Illich, *Energy and Equity* (New York: Harper and Row, 1974).

4   Tadzio Mueller, "Green New Deal: Dead End or Pathway beyond Capitalism?," *Turbulence*, vol. 5, December 2009, http://turbulence.org.uk/turbulence-5/green-new-deal/.

is in fact the century of pain, misery and corruption."[5] Little else can be said for the twentieth century. Indeed, the age of transport has forced us to work even more; after all, constant movement needs to be paid for. If we consider the wage labor necessary to afford a car, it doesn't carry us further than eight kilometers an hour.[6] Lafargue criticized the right to work as an actual enforcement of misery; we have to criticize the right to transport in the exact same way.

If we don't end the age of transport soon, it will end itself. Whether it will be the ecological system that collapses first or another doesn't matter. According to the Danish group Hedonistisk Aktion, we are already past the final stop sign and can therefore happily continue to step on the accelerator and have as much fun as possible: "The inevitability of the apocalypse includes a hitherto neglected potential for a festive global revolt."[7]

There is certainly something attractive about this sentiment. Having fun until the very last moment sounds all right. At the same time, such a radical notion of "no future" has its limits, as it lacks the second part of John Connor's meditations in *Terminator 2*: "The future is not set. There is no fate but what we make for ourselves."

We haven't reached the point of no return yet. It is not guaranteed that the climate and the natural resource crisis will lead to the apocalypse. We don't want to give up the will to form our future. The big challenge consists in leaving the age of

---

5   Paul Lafargue, *The Right to Be Lazy and Other Studies* (Chicago: Charles H. Kerr, 1883), quoted from https://www.marxists.org/archive/lafargue/1883/lazy/.

6   Mugyenyi and Engler, *Stop Signs*, 17.

7   Hedonistisk Aktion, "Apokalypso," *Openhagen*, December 19, 2009, https://web.archive.org/web/20120402184324/http://openhagen.net/blog/article/apokalypso.

transport behind and diving into a post-fossil world where our well-being is not dependent on the destruction of the earth's natural resources. It is a challenge that requires collective decisions on what we want to use nonfossil energies for. If we make the right decisions, the festive revolt might last forever.

Transport must fulfill a purpose; it must not be a purpose in itself. From meaningless, repetitive, enforced, and fossil movement to a hedonistic, lively, rhythmic, and self-determined one. *From the car to the dance floor.*

"Nobody Wins Unless Everybody Wins"

From Jack Kerouac to Bruce Springsteen, pop culture is full of men who celebrate the car and the alleged freedom it brings. The notion of flight embedded in this is apparently very seductive. The automobile's status in pop culture has much to do with the fact that this history has been written mainly by men. For a man, the car might very well represent freedom as it allows fleeing from one's responsibility for the home and the family. The car symbolizes the male genius's dream of independence. It is a dream that pop culture reproduces without end. In her text "A Plea for the Boring Principle of Responsibility," Isobel Hadley-Kamptz summarizes the problematic aspects of this dream aptly:

> The romantic idea of the tortured male genius has always required very specific circumstances, namely the existence of other people, mostly women—wives, mothers, maids, secretaries, lovers—who take care of all the daily responsibilities the tortured genius is incapable of taking care of: someone else has to type the handwritten notes, someone

else has to prepare the meals, someone else has to take care
of the children, and so on. . . . Hidden behind the romanticism of the tortured genius lies an extreme form of individualism: nobody needs anybody else. This romanticism exists
despite the genius's actual helplessness. . . . It is the principle
of responsibility, not that of irresponsibility, that demands
respect for our fellow human beings and our environment.[8]

The existence of the tortured male genius requires the
responsibility of women in the same way the freedom of the
motorist requires mass traffic. As we have seen, mass traffic also
limits the freedom of the motorist, and here we find another
parallel to the alleged freedom of the male genius: in both cases,
it is assumed that freedom is not for everyone since the freedom
of some people requires the lack of freedom of others. The flight
symbolized by the car is an attempt to reach a freedom that can
never be reached since it always robs others of theirs. In game
theory, this is called a zero-sum game: one wins what someone
else loses.

Bruce Springsteen is one of pop culture's most notorious
automobile romantics. His first great hit was called "Born to
Run." The song was a homage to the automobile as a key to
freedom—or at least that's how it was perceived. If we look at
the text a little more closely, we can hear darker tones despite
the glockenspiel and saxophones:

> The highway's jammed with broken heroes
> on a last chance power drive

---

8   Isobel Hadley-Kamptz, "En appell för det tråkiga ansvarstagandet,"
Isobels text och verkstad, October 14, 2009, http://isobelsverkstad.
blogspot.com/2009/10/en-appell-for-det-trakiga.html.

Everybody's out on the run tonight
but there's no place left to hide

Springsteen wrote "Born to Run" when he was twenty-four years old. He has explained that the song was about fleeing, both from oneself and from a specific place. Fifteen years later, the song conveyed a different message when Springsteen performed it on stage. The "muscle rock" was gone and the poetic belief in the freedom provided by the car had mellowed down. In 1988, Springsteen announced the song with the following words: "The individual freedom in itself, without connection to your community, your family and your friends, ends up being empty and meaningless. I realized that those people I put in that car fifteen years ago were out there trying to make a connection."[9]

9   Bruce Springsteen, *Chimes of Freedom* EP (1988).

A song long considered the ultimate anthem of flight was suddenly about the search for human connection, for community. It gives one hope to see the man who has possibly written more songs about driving than any other realize that the freedom provided by the car doesn't come without conditions. But what does this realization mean? Is there no need for flight? Or do we not properly understand what we want to flee from? Perhaps there exists a collective need for flight, instead of an individual need to flee from responsibility? Perhaps what we really want to flee from is a collective lack of power?

If the primary motivation of flight is to get from point A to point B, the car can also be replaced by the train. This is a tempting change of perspective: the train as a social place on the way to an integrated society replaces the nonplace of the car. We would no longer see flight as the only option; instead, we would get motivated to build a better society here and now. Springsteen himself seems to have developed in that direction. In his song "Land of Hope and Dreams," the train symbolizes a collective flight that goes hand in hand with the creation of community:

> *This train / Carries saints and sinners*
> *This train / Carries losers and winners*
> *This train / Dreams will not be thwarted*
> *This train / Faith will be rewarded*
> *This train / Hear the steel wheels singin'*
> *This train / Bells of freedom ringin'*

These are beautiful words. But the train does not qualify as a symbol for collectivity only because we (at least so far) share carriages with other people. Collectivity is not about being at the same place at the same time but about changing it together, about valuing diversity, and about making common decisions.

In a text titled "The Biopolitics of the Subway," the blogger Guldfiske contends that today's public transport system follows a strictly one-dimensional logic: "The subway is a strange public space. You cannot stop anywhere to chat or just hang out. The space reserved for the subway exists exclusively to transport masses of people as effectively as possible from one point to another. This demands permanent control."[10]

If we want to use public transport for a collective flight leaving no one behind and promising a better future for all, the current public transport system needs to be thoroughly changed. But how can this change be achieved? How can we overcome public transport's one-dimensional logic and the model of discipline that comes with it? How can we get all the bodies hauled around the city every day to move in plenty of directions?

In his dissertation *Other Worlds, Other Values*, Tadzio Mueller also writes about Planka.nu. He describes the P-kassa (our solidarity fund insuring fare-dodgers against fines) and our work in general with theoretical concepts borrowed from Gilles Deleuze and Félix Guattari. Mueller suggests that fare-dodging can be seen as an attempt to escape. He uses the term "line of flight" to describe fare-dodging as "a movement which interrupts or suspends familiar, confining, formal possibilities and their prescribed organic and social requirements . . . a movement out of which the

---

10 "Tunnelbanans biopolitik," *Guldfiske*, February 16, 2010, http://guldfiske.se/2010/02/16/tunnelbanans-biopolitik/.

participating bodies are drawn along new vectors in experimental ways."[11]

In this sense, fare-dodging can be seen as a flight from a public transport system subjected to the dictates of one-dimensionality, control, and price. The term "line of flight" is a tool to describe the attempt of crashing the fences that the economic order has built around public space. In the case of public transport, the price and the duty of payment mark the fence, and fare-dodging the possibility to crash it. But an escape alone is not enough. Something new has to be created at the same time. A line of flight must not be understood as something entirely negative (movement *from* something); it must also entail something positive (movement *toward* something). A line of flight entails two parallel activities: while we remove ourselves from certain contexts, we build new ones.

As an individual form of resistance, a line of flight cannot create new collectives. This is also true for fare-dodging. When some of us make the individual choice to ride without a ticket, the duty of payment, the barriers, and the control mechanisms don't disappear. An individual line of flight soon disappears into nothingness. It may momentarily open a door, but the door is soon shut again. This is why Mueller stresses that individual lines of flight have to be linked to others. He says that "the danger of a line of flight is that it may fail to connect with other lines and become pure destruction . . . reduced to drawing 'a pure, cold line of abolition.'"[12]

If all of our individual escape attempts are really about a collective desire to flee disempowerment, how does this relate

11 Tadzio Mueller, *Other Worlds, Other Values: Alternative Value Practices in the European Anticapitalist Movement* (PhD thesis, University of Sussex, 2006), 48.

12 Ibid., 50.

to the automobile? The motorist's line of flight comes in direct conflict with the lines of flight of others. Sorrow soon takes over and the escape becomes a zero-sum game exactly because of the disempowerment one attempts to flee from. The motorist's line of flight cannot connect with others and can therefore never become strong and long-lasting.

Even if it is understandable, fare-dodging as an individual act is not progressive; it is but a momentary challenge to the ruling order. Only when individual lines of flight—the lonely daily cries by thousands of bodies in public transport—connect with others can new and progressive social contexts emerge. Only then can we begin to envision and form alternatives to a public transport system that controls us and limits our movements.

A collective escape from the constraints of the duty of payment is one of the main hopes we have in connection with the P-kassa. We want to bring individual lines of flight together; we want to make meetings possible; we want to make alternatives tangible. Wherever the coming together of individual lines of flight makes new forms of collectivity possible, an alternative to the current social order—which is reflected in the order of public transport—begins to take shape. Nobody is free before all are free. Nobody wins unless everybody wins.

High-Speed Society

"One day, I would like to have a word with Ronnie Peterson and Kenny Bräck and all the race car drivers in their pathetic toy cars who destroy everything around them only because they think they can drive fast when and wherever they want."
—Sara Stridsberg

Our culture's obsession with speed is fascinating. Although it is evident that speeding kills, everyone keeps on doing it. Everything has to move faster and faster. We need cars with more horsepower and with dashboards promising rides beyond speed limits. Who hasn't heard the complaints about boring old social democratic Sweden and its refusal to abolish speed limits on motorways? At least the race car drivers on TV can live out our high-speed dreams; dreams that are as compelling as ever despite everyone being aware of the consequences: rising fuel consumption, more CO_2 emissions, fatal crashes. But shall this stop us from racing? Must we say goodbye to the highest form of freedom?

The real question at this point is the following: If speeding is the highest form of freedom, what is freedom really worth? And what kind of freedom forces us to work ever more so that we can move ever faster? What kind of freedom leads to our workplaces moving farther and farther from our homes— which forces us to move even faster?

High-speed society may manifest itself most clearly in our fascination with airplanes and high-speed trains. We will look more closely at both soon. First, a clarification: it is dangerous to formulate a critique of high-speed society with the help of romantic references to "slowness" or "authenticity." Yes, one may take local trains rather than express trains or indulge in slow food rather than fast food. But neither is a true "choice," because most people cannot afford the luxury to make such choices; most people are at the mercy of high-speed society and the only choice they have is to hang on as tightly as they can. They are forced to commute to work under a lot of stress and to eat disgusting food at gas stations—everything to save time.

There is no individual emergency break other than burning out. Unless the entire train comes to a standstill, we will all be forced to hop on. People of certain professions, academics and freelancers for example, may be able to afford longer journeys on local trains, but to think that individual choices of that kind will beget social movements is ridiculous. The only emergency brake that counts is the collective one, the one that says: *No one is going to continue this journey!*

High-Speed Trains

Today, high-speed trains are hailed by many as the number one solution to the transport problem: fast, efficient, and socially as well as ecologically sustainable. Among the advocates of high-speed trains are a majority of the political parties and all sorts of climate, environment, and community activists.[1] The goals are to make high-speed trains a more attractive option than airplanes, especially on domestic routes, and to diminish

---

1   Karin Svensson Smith, "Höghastighetståg är vägen till framtiden," *Dagens Nyheter*, January 14, 2010, http://www.dn.se/opinion/debatt/hoghastighetstag-ar-vagen-till-framtiden-1.1026440.

car traffic. But there are a number of problems involved. If we take a step back and think about it all pragmatically instead of lapsing into premature euphoria, we can easily see that even if high-speed trains have advantages, they are in no way a solely positive contribution to the transport system.

Let's use the discussion about a high-speed rail network in Sweden as an example. One of the main arguments of its proponents is—just like anywhere else—efficiency: high-speed trains can make journeys, for example the one from Stockholm to Gothenburg, faster. At face value this seems convincing. There is nothing wrong with making it faster to the Gothenburg harbor or to Grandma in Stockholm, is there? And with a clean ecological conscience, too. Yet it seems legitimate to wonder how much of a difference this really makes. Depending on whose calculations we can trust, a high-speed train would save us anywhere between ten and forty-five minutes on this route. For people who only travel on occasion for pleasure, that's not all that much. What the high-speed frenzy really is all about is making it possible to commute to work from Stockholm to Gothenburg and vice versa. Once that is possible, people will feel forced to do it when the opportunity arises—and if they won't, the

employment agency will make sure they do. This stands in complete contrast to positive urban development, which needs to overcome the separation of duties and the necessity of covering ever-longer distances.

No matter whether it is by train or not, forcing people to travel ever-longer distances is not the way to save natural resources and halt climate change. Not to even mention how tiresome it is to have to commute to work four hours every day. The high-speed train is a product of the age of transport. It belongs to the ideology of the twentieth century. If we really want things to change, we need other ideas.

Climate-Smart or Simply Dumb?

High-speed trains are faster than regular trains and ecologically more sustainable than airplanes. These are truisms. But they don't necessarily mean that we have to build high-speed trains. The planned high-speed rail networks shall exist for at least one hundred years. That's a long time. Must we not investigate the most probable consequences very carefully? Must we not look into possible alternatives? Projects like Förbifart Stockholm have been criticized for being planned without considering alternatives. The critique is justified, but it also applies to high-speed trains. Even a government commission came to the conclusion that possible alternatives to high-speed trains were never considered before the latter were propagated as the solution to our transport problems.[2]

---

2   Statens institut för kommunikationsanalys (SIKA), "Remissvar på Banverkets huvudrapport 'Svenska höghastighetsbanor' med bilagor," October 13, 2008, http://www.sika-institute.se/ Doclib/2008/Remisser/re_20081013.pdf; Statens väg- och transportforskningsinstitut (VTI), "Remiss av Banverkets rapport

In current transport planning, one often hears the phrase "avoid—shift—improve." It is a response to any big development project—and the idea of traveling itself—having ecological costs. In Sweden, government agencies subscribed to a "four-step principle" in the early 2000s, which echoes the "avoid—shift—improve" approach. According to the four-step principle, there are four possible steps for resolving transport-related problems; the earlier a viable solution can be found the better:

1. reducing the need for transport and strengthening socially and ecologically sustainable means of transport;

2. making use of existing road and rail networks and their infrastructure;

3. authorizing minor reconstruction projects;

4. authorizing major reconstruction projects and development.

The way in which the government has handled the high-speed train issue clearly violates this. Major development projects were planned without considering any of the other options.

If we are so excited about high-speed trains being better than airplanes, it is only because we remain locked in the age of transport. It is business as usual. The arguments of the

om Svenska höghastighetsbanor," October 9, 2008, http://www. vti.se/epibrowser/svenska%20h%C3%B6ghastighetsbanor.pdf; Regeringskansliet, "Remissammanställning avseende Utredningen om höghastighetsbanors betänkande Höghastighetsbanor—ett samhällsbygge för stärkt utveckling och konkurrenskraft" (SOU 2009:74), December 18, 2009, http://www.regeringen.se/content/1/c6/13/81/51/1660d3f5.pdf.

high-speed train enthusiasts confirm this: "The current rail network is under too much pressure," they say, or: "We need to transport more goods by rail." If we approach these issues not only from the angle of efficiency but also from an environmental one, it is clear that business as usual—that is, an ongoing rise of transporting people and goods—is not sustainable, regardless of the exact form it takes.

In the last decade, at least two comprehensive studies exploring the significance of various social factors for global warming were published in Sweden: *Tvågradersmålet i sikte?* (Is the Two-Degree Solution in Sight?), published by the government's Bureau for Environmental Protection, and *Europe's Share of the Climate Challenge*, published jointly by the Stockholm Environment Institute and Friends of the Earth Europe.[3] Both studies reached very similar conclusions: not even the most optimistic technological outlook allows the assumption that the climate issue can be resolved if the volume of traffic increases at the same rate as it has in recent decades. Now, what does this mean for high-speed trains? After all, high-speed trains will inevitably increase the distances traveled on a regular basis. The expansion of traffic options always leads to more traffic. Not only because it offers people more options to travel but also because the investments need to pay off—in the case of a high-speed rail network in Sweden, we are talking about $15 billion.

Let's consider the ideal case: the high-speed rail network is built and high-speed trains replace many domestic flights, much

3   Naturvårdsverket, "Tvågradersmålet i sikte?," 2007, http://www.naturvardsverket.se/Documents/publikationer/620-5754-1.pdf; Stockholm Environment Institute & Friends of the Earth Europe, "Europe's Share of the Climate Challenge," 2009, http://sei-international.org/?p=publications&task=view&pid=1318.

of automobile traffic, and a fair amount of conventional train traffic. Still, our future wouldn't look any brighter. Too many of the fundamental problems of our transport system would remain. The high-speed rail network would be affected by the scarcity of resources predicted in all areas. *Peak everything.* Peak oil is only the best-known example. With a future energy crisis being inevitable, we need means of transport that aren't only climate-smart but that also help us save energy. Nothing advertised as "high-speed" can do this. An increase in speed means an increase in energy use. There are no exemptions from this rule. Per Kågesson, who studies the connections between ecological systems and energy use, claims that high-speed trains would increase the energy use of the Swedish railway system by at least 60 percent.[4] In addition to this, enormous quantities of oil, steel, and copper will be needed to adjust trains, stations, and other parts of the railway system. And we don't even want to go into the ecological consequences of building new railway lines . . .

So, the government proposes to build a high-speed rail network for $15 billion, and we must not forget that the budgets for projects of this magnitude are almost always exceeded. Think of all the things that could be done with this kind of money if it was used to improve public transport. There is no doubt that the latter must be the priority if our aim really is to reduce, as efficiently as possible, the ecological damage caused by the transport sector.

A European train corridor is one of the prospects that gets high-speed train enthusiasts excited. In Sweden, however, this

---

4   Per Kågesson, "Environmental Aspects of Inter-City Passenger Transport, Discussion Paper," *International Transport Forum*, 2009, http://www.oecd-ilibrary.org/transport/the-future-for-interurban-passenger-transport/environmental-aspects-of-inter-city-passenger-transport_9789282102688-17-en.

is hardly relevant, because there won't be any high-speed trains crossing Denmark.[5] For this reason alone it is more sensible to focus on other things if you want to reach the European continent by train: better services, lower prices, and more night trains.

How about the cheap flights replaced by high-speed trains? Of course, we have nothing against limiting air travel. But what exactly would it mean to replace cheap flights with high-speed trains under current circumstances? In the first place, it would make long-distance travel much more expensive and exclude many people who cannot afford high-priced train tickets from the possibility of long-distance travel altogether. The Swedish government says that high-speed trains would not increase the cost of train tickets. Apart from the fact that the cost of train tickets is very high as it is, this promise is not very credible. Lars Hultkrantz, professor of national economy, considers it to be completely unrealistic, and even an investigative commission appointed by the government had to confirm this.[6] Routes where high-speed trains are already operating, for example between Paris and Brussels, show that conventional train traffic has practically collapsed. People who cannot afford to take high-speed trains must now make their way with local trains, which is very slow and requires numerous transfers. True, businesspeople and EU bureaucrats now often take the train and continue their crazy commutes with good ecological conscience—but is this really what we envision by climate-smart transport for all?

---

5   "Höghastighetsbanor—ett samhällsbygge för stärkt utveckling och konkurrenskraft, betänkande av Utredningen om höghastighetsbanor," SOU 2009:74, 14.9.2009, http://www.regeringen.se/rattsdokument/ statens-offentliga-utredningar/2009/09/sou-200974/.

6   Ibid., 324.

Drive and Fly to Never-Never Land

In April 2010, we spent a few beautiful spring nights on EtherPad to study air traffic: the myth of freedom attached to it, its ecological consequences, and its relation to automobility and high-speed society. Suddenly, something entirely unforeseen happened: from one day to the next, there was an almost complete ban on air traffic across Europe. Our wildest dreams had come true.

The emergency situation that followed revealed a whole number of things, one of which was that organizing human societies without air traffic seemed utterly possible. It became clear that we can survive without the airplane, one of the age of transport's most formidable inventions. Of course, the costs had to be carried by ordinary people and small enterprises. This is common when something occurs that's as sudden and unannounced as the outbreak of the Eyjafjallajökull volcano. Hotels don't reimburse private bookings if you don't arrive in time and employers don't compensate for lost income if you make it home too late and miss work. Meanwhile, companies without the resources required to adapt to the extraordinary circumstances are forced to stop operating. Still, everyday life continued pretty much as usual, despite everyone being in shock. Yes, some folks might have shed a tear over the lack of fresh lemongrass, which prevented them from preparing the Thai chicken curry they had learned to make on Ko Samui,[7] but, all considered, the experience gave us plenty of hope: getting rid of the airplane seemed easier than expected and promised

---

7   Josefine Hökerberg, "Fortsätter stoppet går flygbolagen i konkurs," *Aftonbladet*, April 17, 2010, http://aftonbladet.se/nyheter/article6972064.ab.

various interesting social developments. Of course, airlines are not looking forward to further volcano eruptions or other events downing air traffic, but at the end of the day, our climate seems more important than the well-being of airlines.

Some months after the Eyjafjallajökull eruption, the Swedish airline lobby group Svenskt Flyg initiated a debate on air travel. Maria Rankka from the neoliberal think tank Timbro also got involved not mincing her words. The headline read, "Resistance to flying is class contempt!" Rankka compared the demand for higher fees and taxes for air traffic with travel bans enforced by dictatorships. For her, a critical view on air traffic was akin to expressing hostility toward foreigners and migration.[8]

Timbro's intellectuals might think whatever they want. We are still facing an energy crisis, and our energy use must not only become more effective but, first and foremost, it must decrease. In this context, air traffic does not recommend itself as a means of mass transportation, since no other kind of transportation requires more energy. The fact that the current level of air traffic cannot be reconciled with the climate goals of the Swedish government almost becomes a detail in this context.[9]

It is surprising how difficult it seems for some people to keep two thoughts in their head at the same time. To take the energy and climate crisis seriously means that air traffic has to lose its superior status within the traffic power structure (flying is the only means of mass transportation that is not

---

8   Maria Rankka, "Flygmotståndet är klassförakt," *Newsmill*, February 16, 2010, http://www.newsmill.se/artikel/2010/02/16/flygmotst ndet r-klassf-rakt.

9   Peter Larsson, "Flygets gräddfil måste ses över," *Nyheter från KTH*, February 14, 2011, https://www.kth.se/aktuellt/nyheter/flygets-graddfil-maste-ses-over-1.78448.

taxed). That's one thought. The other is that cheap flights have expanded the leisure opportunities for a large segment of the European working class. We know that. But even if cheap flights have brought advantages for the working classes in rich countries, most people on this planet will never be able to fly regularly, if at all. Still, according to Timbro, questioning flying means questioning human freedom and the right of movement.

It is very bold of Timbro to presume the role of defender of the Swedish working class. If the chatter about "class contempt" was serious, Timbro would fight for sustainable means of transport that are affordable even for low-income people. A class-conscious climate and energy politics does not consist of defending air traffic but of creating practical alternatives—for everyone.

A Strange Kind of Freedom

What kind of freedom does flying promise? We have already addressed the paradox that the myth of freedom linked to the automobile goes hand in hand with an enormous apparatus of social control. The same is true for the airplane. Flying also entertains a myth of freedom, but airplanes and airports are subjected to even stricter rules and regulations than cars and motorways (even if that seems hardly possible). You are told what you are allowed and not allowed to eat and drink; your baggage is scanned and searched; the content of your hand luggage—and therefore your private life—is exposed to complete strangers; your body is stripped, searched, ushered through security checks, and forced to undergo biometric personal identification. Soon even our intentions and thoughts will be registered in the form of psychophysical indicators of stress and anxiety (body temperature, breath, heart rhythm) and compared to the indicators "characteristic for terrorists."[10] Meanwhile, the constant reminders on airports to watch your luggage create an atmosphere of fear and uncertainty. Why did that man leave his bag? Why is the metal detector peeping? Why is the staff looking so skeptical? Have I done something wrong? Is the person next to me a pickpocket? Is the person over there a bomb smuggler? It is not only "suspicious" behavior or luggage that leads to the interference of the security forces, but what you say can also be used against you. The British sociologist Steve Woolgar has pointed out that airports are among the few places in the world where a joke can get you straight into a jail cell.[11]

---

10 Allison Barrie, "Homeland Security Detects Terrorist Threats by Reading Your Mind," *Fox News*, September 23, 2008, http://www.foxnews.com/story/0,2933,426485,00.html.

11 Christopher Kullenberg, "Flyg, diagram & fylum och Woolgar," *Intensifier*, August 24, 2008, http://christopherkullenberg.se/?p=234.

The control apparatus doesn't end at the airport, however. It follows you during the entire journey, into the very last corner of the airplane. Lights above your head and speaker announcements tell you what to do: *Get up! Sit down! Fasten your seat belt! Order something to drink! Eat! Look out of the window when the captain describes the view!* Each moment is prescribed and the only possibility to have a pleasant journey is to adapt. In light of the inhumane build of airplane seats, however, finding yourself strapped to the floor might not be that bad an option.

Due to the self-discipline required, the philosopher of science Christopher Kullenberg describes airplane journeys aptly as an experience of constant discomfort.[12] If we take the Timbroists by word, however, flying is the ultimate experience of freedom. It seems hard to imagine that they really believe this themselves. Then again, maybe they do, since even the former Swedish transport minister Åsa Torstensson hailed flying as pure freedom.[13] This raises an interesting question: What kind of freedom is compatible with a control apparatus that would be unthinkable anywhere else?

Air traffic advocates usually can't explain why they seem to consider airplane journeys to the Canary Islands or Cyprus more valuable than train journeys to Bulgaria or Spain. It is also curious that most of them are staunch defenders of the free market, since air traffic is given advantages in the traffic power structure that render any notion of a "free market" absurd. In any case, our holiday habits will need to change in light of

---

12 Christopher Kullenberg, "Om vemod och tåg," *Intensifier*, October 3, 2009, http://christopherkullenberg.se/?p=1099.

13 Åsa Torstensson, "För mig är flyget ren och skär frihet," *Newsmill*, February 19, 2010, https://web.archive.org/web/20130207231851/ http://www.newsmill.se/artikel/2010/02/19/f-r-mig-r-flyget-ren-och-sk-r-frihet.

the energy and climate crisis. Luckily, flying has never been the only way to travel and relax, and it will never be. There is freedom beyond the airplane.

The future demands that we develop a new understanding of time. It is up to us to realize the full potential of such an understanding. To travel far might take longer. But the additional time we need can easily be won by cutting down on all the traveling we have to do in our daily lives. Working fewer hours and commuting shorter distances in order to free time for a longer train journey hardly means losing quality of life. Rather, it is something that we all will benefit from.

Once the duration of a journey corresponds to the distance covered, we will also experience our surroundings in a new way. Covering long distances with high speed makes us oblivious to many things. Wolfgang Sachs describes this well in his book *For Love of the Automobile*: "For the gaze greedy for distance, the living space of the immediate vicinity degenerates into mere thoroughfares, into a dead space between the beginning and the end; the point is to overcome this space with the least possible loss in time."[14]

Sachs's book is a cultural history of driving. Many aspects apply to flying as well. Everything close by seems hardly worth our attention; all that counts is the promise waiting on the horizon. The cult of automobility causes us to forget the forest behind our house, the lake a bicycle ride away, or the local neighborhood bar featuring talented bands. We need a

---

14 Wolfgang Sachs, *For Love of the Automobile: Looking Back into the History of Our Desires* (Berkeley: University of California Press, 1992), 190.

drastic change of priorities: accessibility must be worth more than mobility. Everything of importance for our lives must be accessible locally. Constant movement must not be required to satisfy our needs.

Working hours cannot be reduced and adequate local holiday options cannot be created without fundamental social change. Luckily, there exist inspiring historical examples. When, thanks to the workers' movement, everyone in Sweden earned the right to holidays, numerous local possibilities arose. Workers built holiday settlements consisting of picturesque wooden cottages. A particularly beautiful example is the settlement Larsboda Strand in the Stockholm suburb of Farsta. Situated in an oak forest right by Lake Drevviken, it is close to the city, accessible to everyone, and ecologically more sustainable than just about any other holiday destination. Allotment gardens also provide a peaceful oasis for many city residents, allowing them to dig in the earth and enjoy the smells of nature.

In a society worshiping the automobility mammoth, many such oases have been destroyed.[15] Since a densely populated city is in many ways more energy-efficient than a thinly populated one, the principle of "redensification" has become a leitmotif of modern urban planning. Redensification alone, however, will hardly solve our energy problems—especially not when the label is used to build at the wrong places for the wrong reasons.[16] Each construction project has to be planned very carefully to ensure that it will indeed bring advantages in

---

15 Erik Berg, "Förtätning i praktiken," *Approximation*, January 23, 2010, http://approximationer.blogspot.com/2010/01/fortatning-i-praktiken.html.

16 Erik Berg, "Truman City: A Critical Look at the Discourse of Densification," *Carbusters*, April 14, 2010, http://carbusters.org/2010/04/14/truman-city/.

terms of energy use and the environment. Otherwise, it will be Robin Hood turned upside down: a redistribution of wealth from the bottom to the top.[17]

Many of us love urban life, but this doesn't mean that we all get high on concrete and have no need for leisure and holidays. Climate-smart options should be a part of urban life as much as entertainment and social gatherings are. "Class contempt" means not offering any such possibilities. It is particularly ironic that the people who have built their luxury homes on the destroyed holiday dreams of the workers' movement will continue to fly regularly—at any cost.

Both driving and flying lead to a disregard of all the curious details that break the monotony of everyday life. Perception that has to adapt to ever-higher speeds needs a controlled environment for the mind to keep up—an environment facilitating car traffic and therefore standing in direct contrast to one that would be stimulating for pedestrians and bicyclists. Wolfgang Sachs describes how speed affects the relation to our environment:

> Pedestrians (and bicyclists) love the minor and the incidental. They feel good where the buildings wear different faces, where the eye can wander over trees, yards, and balconies, where there are people to meet or watch, where they can linger, join in, and get involved, where a multitude of impressions and stimuli can be had along their short way....

17 Janna Roosch, "Förslaget: utplåna Ingers drömstuga," *Mitt i Söderort Farsta*, February 2, 2010.

The situation is wholly different for drivers: they hate surprises and demand predictability; only drawn-out monotony gives them security; only large billboards can capture their attention; only straight, broad, and uneventful routes guarantee them a quick passage without interruption. The car driver tolerates variety only in the rhythm of kilometers, whereas for the pedestrian, space made to conform to speed is faceless and boring.[18]

The two paradigms cannot be reconciled. Stimulating proximity stands against monotonous automobility. Sadly, our cities are mostly characterized by the latter. They have been destroyed by the separation of duties and urban planning in the wake of SCAFT. Our response to this development must not be to repeat the mistakes that have given way to it in the first place. The principle of redensification, for example, must not become a new model excluding all others. Rather, our response must consist of a diversity of approaches and the understanding that the one-and-only solution does not exist.

Let us return once more to the ash that caused a flying ban across Europe. As we have already seen, life did not come to a standstill, even if some liberals tried to make it look that way. The emergency situation that occurred caused rather an array of intriguing ideas and experiments. This made it clear that a disruption of such proportions posed no threat to society but offered an opportunity. No matter how much the liberal air traffic fetishists rant about "environmental Taliban," the

18 Sachs, *For the Love of the Automobile*, 191–92.

Eyjafjallajökull eruption proved that we are far better equipped for the necessary social transformations than most of us thought.

In Mexico, the term *civil society* can be traced to the aftermath of the earthquake shaking the capital in 1985. When the military was deployed to protect rich enclaves from looting while government aid for the people was not forthcoming, popular anger and frustration soon turned into impressive self-organized solidarity projects. Far-reaching alternatives to state control were established on a grassroots level. We could catch a glimpse of this in the aftermath of the Eyjafjallajökull volcano eruption, too, when social media was widely used to organize transport for stranded travelers.[19] The sociologist Karl Palmås summarized the related message thus: "The great thing with the ash story was that it knocked out an important technological development. And when an important technological development—and the practices related to it—are knocked out, humanity will necessarily move into new directions."[20]

---

19 Karin Thurfjell, "Strandsatta liftar på Facebook," *Svenska Dagbladet*, April 16, 2010, http://www.svd.se/nyheter/inrikes/strandsatta-liftar-pa-facebook_4576139.svd; Martin Gelin, "De sociala medierna visar sin verkliga styrka under flygstoppet," *Newsmill*, April 17, 2010, https://web.archive.org/web/20100420062248/http://www.newsmill.se/artikel/2010/04/17/de-sociala-medierna-visar-sin-verkliga-styrka-under-flygstoppet.

20 Karl Palmås, "Upprymdheten inför det Realas inbrott," *99, our 68*, April 17, 2010, http://www.isk-gbg.org/99our68/?p=406.

Speed and Discipline

"Trust is good; control is better."
—Vladimir Lenin & Ronald Reagan

We have addressed the apparatus of control that
is required by the traffic power structure to function. It puts
means of transport as well as people into different, hierarchi-
cally organized categories. It is important to make these hierarchies visible and to emphasize the class differences entailed
in using certain means of transport. The links between transport and class are essential for the traffic power structure.
Automobiles are mostly driven by white, well-earning, and
middle-aged men traveling alone. Automobiles receive most
of the resources and most of the space available in the traffic
power structure. Referring to a stereotypical motorist has its
problems, but it also serves a didactic purpose: it illustrates how
privileges are divided in our society and how this is expressed
in traffic. Young people are not allowed to drive. Poor people
cannot afford to drive (and often don't earn enough to use
public transport either). Old people cannot cover long distances on foot or by bike. And globally speaking, the citizens of
some countries have the right to travel around the entire globe
while others can hardly leave their home country.

In a book about transport, we cannot avoid raising the question of what the "right to free movement" really means. Both
our cities and our nation-states are characterized by borders
and barriers of all kinds. In the city, it is first and foremost

economic resources that determine the right of movement. This is also true for international travel, but with an added political factor: while people with a Swedish passport can travel just about anywhere they want as long as they economically can afford to, "Fortress Europe" becomes surrounded by ever-higher walls denying people with the wrong (or no) passports that exact same right. Many Europeans choose as holiday destinations countries whose citizens are rejected as refugees at European borders.

In Europe's public transport systems, fare-dodgers and undocumented migrants become victims of the same inspections. This illustrates how closely related the different forms of movement control are. After all, Fortress Europe not only protects its outer borders by walls but also makes ticket inspectors chase "illegal immigrants" in public transport. This proves how strongly migration control, and therefore the denial of the right to free movement, is tied to the traffic power structure.

The traffic power structure does not only deny people the right to move between different countries, however. Given economic realities, it also denies the majority of the world's population the use of two of the most valued means of transport: the automobile and the airplane. The fact that neither of them is in any way climate-smart confirms that the lifestyle propagated in the West, inseparable from the automobility paradigm, is the reason for the current climate crisis. The main victims of this crisis, of course, are those excluded from Western societies. Meanwhile, global warming causes them to flee their home countries in ever-greater numbers.[1]

---

1   Ian Traynor, "EU Told to Prepare for Flood of Climate Change Migrants," *The Guardian*, March 10, 2008, http://www.guardian.co.uk/environment/2008/mar/10/climatechange.eu.

The Security-Industrial Complex

We were invited to a conference in Prague. The journey itself was no big deal. Flying around Europe on low-cost airlines has become a very popular way of killing time. The journey got interesting, though, once we paid attention to the details.

The day began with us boarding a subway train on the out-skirts of Stockholm. To reach the platform we had to jump over a security gate installed by the Gothenburg-based company Gunnebo.[2] Luckily, no policemen chasing undocumented migrants were in sight. We saw other passengers opening the gate with their new Access card, which saves all of your travel information and can at any time be consulted by the police (and they do consult it). Once on the platform, we were filmed by cameras installed by Dimension Data, the security-indus-trial branch of Asia's biggest telecommunications marketer NTT.[3] Once on the subway train, we observed security guards working for a company called Securitas providing us with a sense of "safety." Crossing the bridge into the inner city, we saw cameras that IBM installed above the car lanes, register-ing license plate numbers to ensure everyone was going to pay the congestion toll. The same cameras are used to monitor people on the streets of big cities such as New York.[4] Before we

2   "Gunnebo tecknar avtal med AB Storstockholms Lokaltrafik (SL)," *Pressmeddelande från Gunnebo AB*, April 10, 2002, http://news.cision. com/se/gunnebo/r/gunnebo-tecknar-avtal-med-ab-storstockholms-lokaltrafik--sl--om-leverans-av-ny-typ-av-entresparrar-till-ett-varde-av-cir,c57959.

3   "SL:s nya nätverk ökar tryggheten för tunnelbaneresenärer," *Pressmeddelande från Dimension Data och SL*, December 1, 2006, http://news.cision.com/se/dimension-data-sverige/r/sl-s-nya-natverk-okar-tryggheten-for-tunnelbaneresenarer,c245798.

4   "Ett lyckat försök i Stockholm," Informationsblad från IBM om

boarded the airport bus, we went into the supermarket to get
something to drink. What awaited us at the entrance? A security gate installed by Gunnebo. At the airport itself, we were
marshaled through Ryanair's control system. When we faced a
wall of security guards, we noticed that they were all Securitas
employees; not a single police officer was in sight. After two
hours of low-cost flying we finally landed in Prague. We got our
luggage, left the international zone of the airport, and entered
the Czech Republic—through a security gate installed by
Gunnebo. During the trip, we had actually discussed Sweden's
role in the war in Afghanistan and the companies profiting from
it. When we later looked into this more closely, we realized
that Gunnebo did not only build security gates to keep people
from using the subway in Stockholm but also made big profits
in war zones.[5]

   This is only one of innumerable stories that can be used to
illustrate the main characteristics of our everyday life: enclo-
sure, control, surveillance, and siege, all courtesy of the security-industrial complex. In his book *Cities under Siege*, Stephen
Graham describes how metropolises in rich countries serve as
laboratories for the development of technologies that are later
exported to war zones in the Global South.[6] But we are more
than guinea pigs. We are part of a war that comes increasingly
closer. After all, the technologies tested in the Global North

   Stockholms biltullar, 2007, http://www.ibm.com/ibm/ideasfromibm/
   se/sv/howitworks/040207/.
5 "Produktblad från Gunnebo AB för Elkosta BLS Defence Barrier K12,"
   http://www.gunnebo.ae/our-offering/perimeter-protection/access-
   control/boom-barriers/barrier-lift-system/Elkosta%20Barrier%20
   Lift%20System.
6 See Stephen Graham, *Cities Under Siege: The New Military Urbanism*
   (London: Verso, 2010).

are not only exported but also used to fortify the borders of Europe. They are used to keep unwanted people out and to suppress unwanted behavior of those already in. It is astounding to observe the many unforeseen ways in which control and surveillance systems tested in Europe are used around the world. The blogger Guldfiske writes: "The gates of the Stockholm subway system now serve a double purpose. They not only regulate access to the subway system but also enforce social segregation. They have become a point of control where the city's bodily streams are easiest to observe and divide. Not only is a valid ticket required but also valid papers and valid behavior."[7]

The metropolis is a terrain of constant conflict. It is not a war zone, but the war is not far away. For a long time, the military avoided the city or confined itself to lay it under siege. Today, the metropolis has become incorporated into the logic of war. Armed conflict is only one aspect of this logic. The rivalries between the superpowers remind of police work. No one is concerned with victory or defeat. The goal is not to establish peace or to (re)establish a particular political order. All activities are simply security operations, and the red thread of the security industry connects Stockholm directly with Baghdad. War has no longer a beginning and an end; it has become a series of micro-actions. There are plenty of examples: laws for monitoring data traffic (with fear-inducing acronyms such as FRA, IPRED, and ACTA); the blurring of boundaries between police, military, border patrol, and private security firms; the machinization of responsibility. A new politics of security has engulfed the globe. An article on the blog *Fragment* outlines the interaction between state and capital in the security-industrial complex:

---

7   "Tunnelbanans biopolitik."

Security has become a commodity. As such it is traded, regardless of whether there is an actual need for it or not. Security firms are driven by profit interests and always on the lookout for new markets. . . . This is not to be understood purely mechanically. It is not like these firms only exist to exploit people's fears. This would be very banal analysis. The security firms are only another effect of security's commodification. It is easy to believe that we must monitor our environment in order to survive.[8]

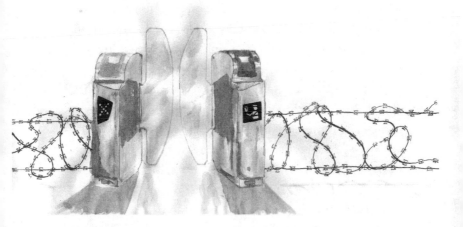

The article sheds light on the problems entailed in nation-states outsourcing the monopoly of violence to private firms, such as Securitas. At the same time, we, the people, are made responsible for our personal safety. All of this despite the fact that we have never been monitored more thoroughly than today. Still, the demands are clear: *Move to a gated community! Demand*

---

8   Fredric Skargren, "Kollektivtrafik under hård press," *Fragment*, September 24, 2010, https://web.archive.org/web/20101017030641/ http://www.frangere.se/2010/09/24/kollektivtrafik-under-hard-press/.

security cameras in your neighborhood! Lock your doors! Report suspicious behavior!

Since 2003 (the same year the invasion of Iraq began), the Department of Homeland Security has been supervising the U.S. security industry. The Department of Homeland Security was founded to strengthen the country's civil defense and to support the military operations led by the Department of Defense. It got access to all of the Bureau of Immigration's data. Soon, the "Homeland Security bubble" became one of the USA's fastest growing industries: "Homeland security may have just reached the stage that Internet investing hit in 1997. Back then, all you needed to do was put an 'e' in front of your company name and your IPO would rocket. Now you can do the same with 'fortress.'"[9]

The companies belonging to the security-industrial complex are not very concerned about security. They are concerned about money. This is why they have no reservations selling you the most useless crap. They are happy when we feel threatened and want to feel "secure." They also make sure that none of their security systems works perfectly in order to guarantee a constant demand for updated versions. The overlapping of profit interests with "heavy-handed politics" forms the foundation of the security-industrial boom we are witnessing today.

Advocates of "rational" and "modern" society are in deep trouble whenever prompted to explain the actual benefits of the security-industrial complex. Neither the wonderful market, which should, as a result of stimulating competition, produce magnificent goods and ensure that all resources go to where they are needed, nor sensible and perceptive liberal-democratic

9   Daniel Gross, "The Homeland Security Bubble," *Slate*, June 1, 2005, http://www.slate.com/id/2119866/.

politics can control their own destructiveness, since everything is determined by the maximization of profits and votes. Politicians always try to look busy even when we'd all benefit from them doing nothing at all. Those who profit from the security-industrial complex know this, and they also know how to use it to their advantage. And we, the ordinary mortals? We are left with reelected governments and debts to the security firms.

In Bruce Schneider's book *Beyond Fear*, the process sketched above is described as a "security theater." The term refers to all of the measures employed to provide a sense of security, without actually making anything more secure. The security theater makes use of the discrepancy between perceived risk and actual risk. Since the actual risk we are in can never justify all of today's security measures, politicians and the security industry have a special interest in perceived risk.[10]

To make this more concrete, we can take a look at the bourgeois politicians responsible for Stockholm's public transport system. They are doing a terrible job. One reason is that they are simply incompetent. Another reason is that they are firm believers in lowering taxes. As a result, there aren't any funds for real improvements. The politicians like to blame the fare-dodgers, of course, while wasting the limited resources they have on more barriers and ticket inspectors. This allows them to appear tough, while it allows the security firms to further fill their bank accounts. Politicians win votes, security firms make profits, and we who ride public transport and finance the security theater lose out.

10 See Bruce Schneier, *Beyond Fear: Thinking Sensibly about Security in an Uncertain World* (New York: Copernicus, 2003).

Automated surveillance systems have everything to offer from highly developed software to sophisticated cameras. They have changed security policies radically. Responsibility is increasingly machinized. In many cases, it is no longer people assessing risks but computer programs. The effect is similar to that of using drones in war: if you search for anyone who is accountable you usually search in vain. The same is true when the question of whether a certain behavior is suspicious or not is left for software developers to decide. In order to write the algorithms of global security, huge amounts of data have to be sifted through. Modern security policies focus on prevention. Data mining is used to produce sociograms supposed to detect undesirable behavior. The choice of adjective here is not random: whether what you do is *criminal* or not can never be known by machines; they only know what is *undesirable*.

Bourgeois politicians and their intellectual lackeys emphasize again and again that there is a connection between Swedish cities and Kabul.[11] They are perfectly right: what is practiced in Kabul is prepared in Sweden. Politicians order, Gunnebo delivers. The state buys, capital profits. We pay and are under surveillance.

The Nuclear Society

Future means of transport are usually discussed under the veil of "neutral technology." Despite all the ecological lip service, crucial questions, such as those about energy sources, are sidelined. No one dares imagine a future without expansion and growth. But the challenges posed by transport can never be

---

11 Claes Arvidsson, "Afghanistan handlar också om Nordstan," *Svenska Dagbladet*, November 1, 2010, http://www.svd.se/opinion/ledarsidan/aghanistan-handlar-ocksa-om-nordstan_5600047.svd.

solved technologically; they have to be solved politically. Any technology used on a wide scale is the result of political decisions. Some protect the doctrine of might is right (the automobile), others promote centralization (the oil industry as well as the nuclear industry). Herbert Marcuse described the problem in *The One-Dimensional Man*: "In the face of the totalitarian features of this society, the traditional notion of the 'neutrality' of technology can no longer be maintained. Technology as such cannot be isolated from the use to which it is put."[12]

The oil industry has made exemplary use of the fact that prioritizing certain technologies can determine social development for decades. André Gorz has explained this in his text "The Social Ideology of the Motorcar":

> The oil magnates were the first to perceive the prize that could be extracted from the wide distribution of the motorcar. If people could be induced to travel in cars, they could be sold the fuel necessary to move them. For the first time in history, people would become dependent for their locomotion on a commercial source of energy. There would be as many customers for the oil industry as there were motorists—and since there would be as many motorists as there were families, the entire population would become the oil merchants'

---

12 Herbert Marcuse, *One-Dimensional Man: Studies in the Ideology of Advanced Industrial Society* (Boston: Beacon, 1964), xvi.

customers. The dream of every capitalist was about to come true. Everyone was going to depend for their daily needs on a commodity that a single industry held as a monopoly.[13]

The dependence on the automobile, and therefore on oil, has made us dependent on an oligopoly consisting of a handful of companies. A technology dependent on oil is necessarily a centralized technology since extracting oil requires a close collaboration of state and capital. This is often overlooked when people discuss the problems of the oil industry. But environmental damage and peak oil are far from the only aspects giving reason for concern. The centralism deriving from our dependence on oil is an enormous political problem, and we need to raise the question of how the oil industry can be replaced.

For people who hold on to the necessity of growth—and hence to increased energy use—nuclear power often appears to be the best solution. For people favoring sustainable energy politics it does not. First, uranium is a limited resource, just like fossil energy. Second, nuclear power is life-threatening and the question of nuclear waste far from resolved.

In the 1970s, a French economist working for the government's energy department wrote a book about nuclear power in which he described nuclear society as a "society of cops." A few days later, he was fired.[14] His argument was that dependence on nuclear energy undermines self-organization. We believe he was right: with all due respect to anarchist cooperatives, the author

---

13 André Gorz, "The Social Ideology of the Motor Car," originally published as "L'ideologie sociale de bagnoleÆ" in *Le Sauvage*, September–October 1973, quoted from http://www.bikereader.com/contributors/misc/gorz.html.

14 André Gorz, *Ecology as Politics* (Boston: South End Press, 1980), 109.

and activist Chris Carlsson asked a fair question when wondering whether we'd really want them to run nuclear power stations.

Although the social consequences of nuclear power are both enormous and obvious, nuclear power is also primarily discussed as a technological problem, not a political one. And yet, even on a technological level it becomes clear how undemocratic nuclear power is, as, again and again, it is explained to us that nuclear power is simply too complicated to leave relevant decisions to laymen.

In the end, all of these questions converge into a fundamental one: What kind of society do we want to live in? Nuclear power is the expression of a specific political ideology. The American physicist Alvin Weinberg compared it with a Faustian pact with the devil: humanity pays for inexhaustible energy with the promise to eternally protect its source.[15] This is the hidden truth of nuclear power: it demands eternal social stability and forces all future societies to adopt the assumptions of the existing one. Oil and nuclear power not only threaten our lives, they threaten the *political foundations* of our lives.

There are numerous possibilities to win energy in ecologically sustainable ways without any need for centralization. This is also true for means of transport. "Green energy" does not suffice as a catchword. The political implications have to be considered: do certain forms of energy require centralism and expertocracy, or do they allow for decentralization and democracy?

The transition to sustainable forms of energy requires the will to radically reduce our energy use. The biggest energy crisis we are facing has nothing to do with peak oil or other resource shortages. It rather concerns our *need* for energy. Let us quote Ivan Illich: "The energy crisis cannot be overwhelmed by more

---

15 Ibid., 108.

energy inputs. It can only be dissolved, along with the illusion that well-being depends on the number of energy slaves a man has at his command. For this purpose, it is necessary to identify the thresholds beyond which energy corrupts, and to do so by a political process that associates the community in the search for limits."[16]

The negative consequences of today's energy use are not only obvious in transport but in agriculture as well. The human ecologist Alf Hornborg argues that if we consider the entire energy used in modern agriculture, and not just the farmer's working hours, modern agriculture is less energy-efficient than preindustrial agriculture was. Twenty years ago, a study came to the conclusion that the output of milk production in England corresponded to only 37 percent of the energy invested in it.[17] Similar numbers apply to car traffic. As we have seen, when we consider the time and effort necessary to own and operate a car, it only carries us eight kilometers an hour.[18]

Demanding to drastically reduce our energy use has nothing to do with technophobia. It is merely based on the insights that an energy crisis can't be avoided and that neutral technology doesn't exist. Some technologies are just bad for us, and it is our common responsibility to choose the ones that aren't. The matter is too important to be left to individual choice. We don't want a society of cops, and we don't want technologies that destroy the foundations of our lives either.

16 Ivan Illich, *Energy and Equity* (London: Marion Boyers, 2009), 22.
17 Erik Berg, "Det ekologiskt ojämna utbytet," *Approximation*, December 15, 2009, http://approximationer.blogspot.com/2009/12/det-ekologiskt-ojamna-utbytet.html.
18 Mugyenyi and Engler, *Stop Signs*, 17.

Suffering in Traffic

"They paved paradise, and put up a parking lot."
    —Joni Mitchell

In this book, we have stressed the principle of accessibility as a guideline for social change. We have also criticized commuting, for three reasons: first, a society built on the permanent transport of goods and labor is extremely energy-intensive; second, the traffic system required by such a society destroys our cities; third, it is very painful to be stuck in commuter traffic during a big part of our day, especially when we don't even get rewarded for it—even though commuting is a part of the workday, it is not treated as such.

For many people, the displeasure they associate with commuting makes them hate traffic altogether. Human happiness has become a much-researched topic in recent years. The *New York Times* wrote that "the daily activities most associated with happiness are sex, socializing after work and having dinner with others. The daily activity most injurious to happiness is commuting."[1]

Many people describe their commute as the worst time of the day. It is a dreadful ritual, which we apparently never get used to. There are tedious routines we can get ourselves prepared for. But with traffic we never know *exactly* what is going to happen. The flow of traffic never stops, but it is never

---

1   David Brooks, "The Sandra Bullock Trade," *New York Times*, March 29, 2010, http://www.nytimes.com/2010/03/30/opinion/30brooks.html.

the same flow. In the words of the psychologist Daniel Gilbert, "traffic is a different kind of hell every day."[2] But commuting is not only a different kind of hell every day. As Goethe already noted, it also has similarities to gambling: there are winners and losers. But who are the winners? And why? And at whose cost?

The cultural geographer Erika Sandow has explored these questions in a study titled *On the Road: Social Aspects of Commuting Long Distances to Work*. It investigates commuting with a special focus on gender relations.[3] The study is highly relevant for the reason alone that the distances covered by commuters in Europe are constantly rising. There are no indications that this trend will end anytime soon. Today, more than 15 percent of EU citizens travel at least two hours to and from work every day. Sandow defines a long-distance commute as forty-five minutes or more one way.

Long-distance commutes can bring advantages to the people enduring them: better jobs, better pay, more fun at work. Long-distance commutes also allow people to keep their homes when they find a new job. Still, commuting has its price, and we don't just mean time. While the advantages of commuting are enjoyed by the commuters themselves (often men), the price is paid by others, especially those living with commuters (often women). In couple households where both partners commute, the person commuting a shorter distance (often a woman) also does most of the housework.

Since 1970, the number of people in Sweden who travel to a different county to work has doubled. Today, the average

2   Jonah Lehrer, "Commuting," *The Frontal Cortex*, March 30, 2010, http://scienceblogs.com/cortex/2010/03/30/commuting/.

3   Siehe Erika Sandow, *On the Road: Social Aspects of Commuting Long Distances to Work* (Umeå universitet: Kulturgeografiska institutionen, 2011), http://www.avhandlingar.se/avhandling/a3da7332e9/.

commuter travels 16.6 km, but 50 percent of all commuters travel less than 8 km. The trend is obvious: some, both men and women, cover ever-longer distances. Men travel farther on average (19.1 vs. 13.7 km), but they don't spend more time traveling since they use cars more often. This essentially means that men have access to a wider labor market.[4]

Even if the differences in commuting between men and women have diminished in recent years, they are far from gone. Sandow explains this as follows:

> Women have continued to be the primary caretakers of household and family obligations. For example, women make several stops and run errands on their way to work more often than men do. Men commute by driving a car more often than women do, while women use public transportation more often. Moreover, women are still mainly employed in low-income occupations, which make long-distance commuting less economically worthwhile and attractive than it is for men with their normally higher-income occupations. Moreover, many women are employed in the public-service sector, in which workplace location can allow a short commuting distance.[5]

As soon as women living with male partners travel longer distances to work, the men take more responsibility for the home and the children. However, the support that men commuting long distances receive from their partners is greater. This is another reason for the gender difference reflected in the average commuting distance:

---

4   Ibid., 8–11.
5   Ibid., 9.

As a consequence, the majority of long-distance commuting women do not feel they have enough support and therefore experience lower family satisfaction and less success in their work role than do short-distance commuting women. . . . As longer commutes reduce the time left for other daily activities, this often results in altered divisions of labour between paid and unpaid work whereby the non-commuting partner (often the woman) reduces his or her working hours and instead shoulders more household-related work. The non-commuting partner thus experiences an economic loss.[6]

Even if commuting allows some people to leave most of the housework to their partners, it does not mean they enjoy it. Studies show that many long-distance commuters suffer from sleep disorders, stress, and general physical as well as psychological discomfort.[7] Even if using public transport instead of the automobile can lessen the symptoms, the problems only disappear once the commuting distance is significantly reduced. The less time people commute, the more time they have to travel to places they actually want to travel to.

Another Look at Positive Psychology

Researchers have revealed connections between commuting and unhappiness. Fine. But how does this kind of research really help us? Karl Palmås writes: "Research about happiness begins with the psychological question about what provides us with a sense of happiness and what doesn't. In clinical psychology,

---

6   Ibid., 19.
7   Ibid., 15–16.

this has led to so-called cognitive behavioral therapy and the marginalization of traditional, 'slow' forms of psychotherapy."[8]

Palmås points at the problems of the "happiness ideology" and its imperatives: *Enjoy! Be free and happy!* He emphasizes that "freedom and happiness do not come from prohibiting people to feel unfree and unhappy." In other words, an obsession with happiness does not eradicate the causes of unhappiness. Nor must the difference between happiness and duty be erased. There are people who claim that we have lost our "sense of duty" and become slaves to hedonism. This is wrong. Rather, happiness has become our duty. Who has never felt the pressure to demonstrate one's happiness with trance-like movements on the dance floor? Who doesn't know the expectation of always being in a great mood and always getting excited about meeting new people? Who has never felt forced to assure others how "incredibly fascinating" their "new projects" are? What once was a desire (*I want to be happy*) has turned into a demand (*I have to be happy*).

In her book *Bright-sided: How the Relentless Promotion of Positive Thinking Has Undermined America*, Barbara Ehrenreich reveals the affirmative character of positive psychology, pointing out that positive psychology assumes that people should, in fact, be happy under the given social circumstances. In this sense, positive psychology confirms the social status quo rather than inspiring people to change it.[9]

Despite the fact that happiness can't be enforced, and despite the conservative tendencies of positive psychology, there is no doubt that we want people to be happy. A first important step

---

8   Karl Palmås, "Från 'är du lönsam, lille vän?' till 'är du lycklig, lille vän?,'" *99, our 68*, April 5, 2010. http://www.isk-gbg.org/99our68/?p=404.

9   See Barbara Ehrenreich, *Bright-sided: How the Relentless Promotion of Positive Thinking Has Undermined America* (New York: Metropolitan Books, 2009).

would be to overcome a strictly individual understanding of happiness (*every man is the architect of his own fortune*). Rather, happiness must be seen as a social project challenging the institutions and structures that produce unhappiness. We can only counteract the teachings of "self-help" prophets and "life coaching" gurus with a concerted and organized effort to overcome anxiety, fear, and pain ourselves. Ehrenreich, too, can imagine a radical version of positive psychology: one that fights for democracy at the workplace and the dismantling of economic gaps in society at large.

If social activism really contributes to happiness and if we take the demand to strengthen a sense of collectivity in our cities seriously, then commuting, especially by car, appears in an even worse light. After all, commuting does not only make the commuters unhappy but everyone affected by the antisocial traffic system that it requires. Neighborhoods adapted to mass traffic have a strong negative impact on social relationships and community-building.

A study, which has demonstrated this more impressively than any other, was conducted by the traffic planner Joshua Hart in Bristol. Hart compared the social relationships among residents along three different roads. The conclusion is simple: the automobile cannot take a leading role in a community without destroying it; in other words, the automobile and community don't go together.

The three roads that Hart chose for his study had very different volumes of traffic: on Dovercourt Road, 140 cars passed daily; on Filton Avenue 8,420 cars; and on Muller Road 21,130 cars. After comprehensive research and many interviews, Hart compiled a chart to illustrate the social relationships along each road: on Dovercourt Road residents had an average of 5.35 friends and 6.1 acquaintances; on Filton Avenue the average was 2.45 friends and

3.65 acquaintances; and on Muller Road, it was 1.15 friends and 2.8 acquaintances. Residents themselves summed this up as follows:

Dovercourt Road: "There is really a sense of community, we look after each other."

Filton Avenue: "It's not so friendly, you barely see anyone."

Muller Road: "People just go from their cars to their houses."[10]

Happiness in Traffic Depends on Happy Traffic

To increase people's happiness is a difficult task. What makes people happy is—luckily—not always the same. Yet, certain things seem to make just about everyone unhappy, car traffic and commuting among them. This should be reason enough to bring about a few changes.

Critiques of the modern city are often underpinned by a longing for something "original" or "genuinely human," something that supposedly existed before all the demolition and reconstruction. We must be careful with such notions even if they are understandable. In our opinion, the problem is not that cities change but that we have no part in this change. This is why many experience demolition and reconstruction as a shock. They react with nostalgia, like Anna-Lena Löfgren in the old hit "Lyckliga gatan" (Happy Street), in which she laments: "Happy street, now you are gone, you have disappeared with the whole neighborhood / Silence has replaced games, silence has replaced songs, and concrete floats above the ground."

---

10 See Joshua Hart, *Driven to Excess: Impacts of Motor Vehicle Traffic on Residential Quality of Life in Bristol, UK* (master's thesis, University of the West of England, 2008), http://www2.grist.org/grist-images/2011/June/6-20/DTESummary.pdf.

Modern urbanites like to ridicule such sentiments, and it is perhaps hard to blame them. But the ridicule can easily become counterproductive when it targets a problem's symptoms rather than addressing its causes. What leads to sentiments like the ones expressed by Löfgren is the feeling of disempowerment that many people experience in times of urban transformation. Instead of taking this feeling seriously, one laughs at those who know no other response but the romanticization of a city they feel they have lost. Ironically, any attempt to appease the nostalgics usually consists of even more "urban development" planned by "experts." The result is the same: the city's residents feel excluded. After all, they want to plan and form their city themselves.

As always, economic interests play a role, too. As soon as "urban development" threatens the value of inner-city apartments (often former public housing flats cheaply acquired in Right to Buy schemes), it becomes unattractive for this reason alone. The key question remains how self-determination and direct democracy can be manifested in an urban development that satisfies the needs and desires of the city's residents. Even if we don't have a simple answer to that question, we are convinced that people must be given more influence in shaping their cities and neighborhoods, so that, to quote Anna-Lena Löfgren once more, "a song arises again one day between these houses, more lovely and beautiful than the one before."

Happiness can neither be prescribed nor commanded. Happiness is formed. It is impossible to determine the exact outcome, but we can make the process much easier by making community, self-management, and participation easier. When we create conditions that allow for social action—both spontaneous and planned—then we create conditions that serve the well-being of the people without telling them what to do.

The Highest Stage
of Liberalism

"Dame más gasolina!"
—Daddy Yankee

We hate cars because car traffic has turned us into slaves to enforced movement—an enforced movement that is liberal and individualistic, and that puts a price tag on our bodies, our labor, and our time. Just as liberalism has handed us meaningless individual choices at the cost of comfort and welfare, the car has handed us mobility at the cost of free movement.

In the age of transport, the market depends on constant mobility. Liberalism takes care of the political framework by forcing us to be flexible, mobile, and lonely. Only when we break the automobility paradigm and determine our movements ourselves will we take our lives into our own hands.

Our primary target is not the automobile itself but the society it creates. Yet the automobile itself is not neutral. It is more than a means of transport or a practical tool allegedly improving our lives and increasing our freedom—it is the basis of mass traffic and responsible for all the costs that come with it.

Mass traffic manifests the absolute rule of liberalism over everyday life. It has created a world in which movement happens in isolation. The idea of the atomic individual is far from natural; it constantly has to be groomed and reproduced. The car is the perfect medium to isolate people from one another, to control them, to make them vulnerable. In car traffic, each individual tries to win at the cost of other individuals. It is a zero-sum game, in which no one can win without someone else losing. A short-cut here or a passing there hands someone an extra minute of time at the expense of someone else's time—or even life.

The disadvantages of mass traffic are all known today, but the illusionary romanticism connected to it is still as strong as it was fifty years ago. Neither alarming research nor depressing reports can do it any harm. The reason for this is the liberal ideology and its special conception of freedom and movement. We have tried to emphasize this by introducing the term *auto-mobility*: independence (*autonomy*) reached by movement (*mobility*)—and movement reached by independence.

Automobility determines not only life on the road. Take a look at the next pedestrian rushing down the street without paying any attention to their surroundings. This is not a human pattern of movement. The pedestrian acts like a motorist. With mass traffic, the principle of automobility has pervaded all social fields. The modern city is built so that each form of movement follows the automobility paradigm. It determines our thinking and controls our societies with the help of an anti-social logic of rationality, separation of duties, speed, purpose, and efficiency. Everyone becomes subjected to the strongest player in the traffic power structure. The social groups faring the worst are those who have always fared the worst. No social hierarchy can be isolated from its social context. Mobility is directly linked to class, gender, and territory. When all social resources are invested in car traffic, humans who cannot afford a car effectively lose their right of movement.

In the automobile society, all other means of transport are worth less. Trains, buses, bicycles, and legs can never compete with the car. This cements the glorious image of the automobile to the point where not even the paradox of promising freedom in the name of control can do it any harm.

When a car occupies a spot in the city, the spot cannot be occupied by any other car. Each parked car hinders all others from parking in the same spot. And when motorists drive too fast, they impact all other motorists, too, since the latter need to be careful not to get hurt.

The twentieth century was the century in which humanity adapted to automobile traffic. Our cities were fundamentally changed in order to satisfy the automobile's needs. The construction (and the extension) of urban highways and parking lots required enormous resources. So did the expansion of traffic laws. Each new road created more traffic, each new parking lot was soon too small, and each SUV forced other motorists to buy even bigger vehicles for their own safety.

A traffic system resting on individualism and speed requires a control apparatus that inevitably puts a limit to what we can do in life. The automobile society has made us dependent on its own implications: we have to take loans to buy cars; we have to work to repay the loans and maintain the cars; we need oil companies to fill our tanks; we need garages for repairs; we need governments to build roads, and so forth. There is no end. The automobile has created the society that liberals have always dreamed of. It has sent us to closed institutions of freedom consisting of endless motorways and isolated shopping malls.

The separation of duties demands that we live in one place, work in another, and have fun in a third. This is a consequence of the automobile society. After all, we can only move between those places somewhat efficiently with a car. We take the car to the fitness center because running in the city is too dirty and inconvenient. On the way to work we gobble down a disgusting sandwich in the driver's seat. And in order to support such misery we work ever-longer hours. Then we long for a holiday—and work even more to be able to afford one.

The constant striving for profit prevents social change that would give our lives meaning, for example the shortening of working hours or the strengthening of lively communities. The dependence on transport is so total that we often forget how absurd it is to drive to the gym in order to exercise or to fly halfway around the world in order to relax. We forget that there are indeed other possibilities.

We sometimes hear that automobile traffic leads to a drive-in society. We can see such tendencies, for example, when more and more social functions are separated from others in order to make the use of the car even more effective. At the same time, this analysis ignores that driving is also a flight from society. The automobile is a private steel bunker on wheels protecting us from other people. Motorists don't have to get off at the same stops, listen to the conversations of other people, smell them, or feel their presence in any other way. The movement of the car happens in isolation. Loneliness. One man per car. If this is freedom, freedom is scary.

In the Berlin district of Kreuzberg, elevators allow motorists to park their cars next to their apartments, even if they live in multi-story buildings. Drivers must not spend a single second on the street dealing with other people. This goes beyond a drive-in society. It is rather a drive-*through* society. Then again, it might no longer be a society at all . . .

Perhaps there is a fear hidden behind our hatred for the car. After all, seeing society disappear induces fear. Society is a place where people have something in common and shape something together. The individualism of automobile traffic undermines this. It creates unnecessary conflict between people who only try to get by. Flipping the finger and cursing are everyday occurrences in traffic. Such outbursts may seem relatively harmless, but in the tabloids we also find worrying new terms such as "parking lot murder."

If we want to fight liberalism, we need to fight automobile traffic. Liberals fear nothing more than collectivization and organizing. Public transport is a powerful weapon against the automobile society. Car traffic makes us lonely and isolates us, public transport creates social connections; car traffic is determined by competition (everyone is trying to take away something from someone else) public transport is a shared space, which improves whenever new people enter it; car traffic locks people in and separates them, public transport brings them together.

It is possible to build a society in which (auto)mobility is no longer a categorical imperative. Of course, this doesn't mean that we will stop moving. It only means that the enforcement of a monotonous back and forth will disappear. We will feel like *a part of society* during our journeys, rather than trying to escape it.

As much as the idea of free individuals choosing their own destinies is the product of a certain society, the idea of automobility is the product of certain politics. A politics that defines not only the framework of automobility but also hides its inner contradiction, namely that the automobility of some depends on the immobility of others. The automobile is only a key to freedom where society has ceased to exist. Just think of all the car commercials featuring empty mountain roads.

Instead of shaping public transport according to the rules of automobile traffic, we must strengthen its collective character; instead of individualizing it, we must emphasize its role as a social meeting place. A first step is taken when we not only tolerate the communal character of public transport but actively embrace it as a means to create a vibrant society.

These days, we regularly hear about "the crisis of the I." This is our response: *Use this crisis to ring in its demise!* Cars are isolated islands, but humans are not. We are organized, our hearts are burning, and soon your cars will be burning, too. *Danos más gasolina!*

About Planka.nu

Planka.nu is a network of local groups fighting for free public transport. It was founded in 2001 in Stockholm, Sweden, by activists from Sweden's Syndicalist Youth Association. Apart from engaging in public debate, direct action, and guerrilla media, the network administers the "P-kassa," a solidarity fund covering fines for people commonly known as fare-dodgers, although they are more aptly described as passengers in public transport engaged in an anti-fare strike.

About PM Press

PM Press was founded at the end of 2007 by a small collection of folks with decades of publishing, media, and organizing experience.

We seek to create radical and stimulating media to entertain, educate, and inspire. We aim to distribute these through every available channel with every available technology, whether that means you are seeing anarchist classics at our bookfair stalls; reading our latest vegan cookbook at the café; downloading geeky fiction e-books; or digging new music and timely videos from our website.

Contact us for direct ordering and questions about all PM Press releases, as well as manuscript submissions, review copy requests, foreign rights sales, author interviews, to book an author for an event, and to have PM Press attend your bookfair:

PM Press • PO Box 23912 • Oakland, CA 94623
510-658-3906 • info@pmpress.org • www.pmpress.org

FOPM: MONTHLY SUBSCRIPTION PROGRAM

Friends of PM allows you to directly help impact, amplify, and revitalize the discourse and actions of radical writers and artists. It provides us with a stable foundation to build upon our early successes and provides a much-needed subsidy for the materials that can't necessarily pay their own way. You can help make that happen—and receive every new title automatically delivered to your door once a month. And, we'll throw in a free T-shirt when you sign up.

Here are your options:
- **$30 a month:** Get all books and pamphlets plus 50% discount on all webstore purchases
- **$40 a month:** Get all PM Press releases (including CDs and DVDs) plus 50% discount on all webstore purchases
- **$100 a month:** Superstar—Everything plus PM merchandise, free downloads, and 50% discount on all webstore purchases

For those who can't afford $30 or more a month, we have **Sustainer Rates** at $15, $10 and $5. Sustainers get a free PM Press T-shirt and a 50% discount on all purchases from our website.

Your Visa or Mastercard will be billed once a month, until you tell us to stop. Or until our efforts succeed in bringing the revolution around. Or the financial meltdown of Capital makes plastic redundant. Whichever comes first.